The GROW UP Challenge Devotional:

A 6-Step Guide to Spiritual Growth

K.A. Baskin-Springer

The GROW UP Challenge Devotional: A 6-Step Guide to Spiritual Growth

Copyright © 2025 by K.A. Baskin-Springer

All rights reserved.

No part of this publication may be reproduced, distributed, stored in a retrieval system, or transmitted in any form or by any means, including photocopying, recording, or other electronic or mechanical methods, without the prior written permission of the author, except as permitted by the United States of America copyright law. For permission requests, write to thegrowupchallenge@kabaskinspringer.com

1st Edition

ISBN: 979-8-9937309-0-5 (paperback)
ISBN: 979-8-9937309-2-9 (ebook)

Printed in the United States of America

Scripture quotations marked "AMP" are taken from the Amplified® Bible, Copyright © 1954, 1958, 1962, 1964, 1965, 1987 by The Lockman Foundation. Used by permission. www.Lockman.org

Scripture quotations marked "ASV" are taken from the American Standard Version Bible (Public Domain).

Scripture quotations marked "BSB" are taken from The Holy Bible, Berean Standard Bible. BSB is produced in cooperation with Bible Hub, Discovery Bible, OpenBible.com, and the Berean Bible Translation Committee. This text of God's Word has been dedicated to the public domain.

Scripture quotations marked "BLB" are taken from The Holy Bible, Berean Literal Bible, BLB. Copyright ©2016, 2018 by Bible Hub. Used by Permission. All Rights Reserved Worldwide. www.berean.bible

Scripture quotations marked CSB have been taken from the Christian Standard Bible®, Copyright © 2017 by Holman Bible Publishers. Used by permission. Christian Standard Bible® and CSB® are federally registered trademarks of Holman Bible Publishers.

Scripture quotations marked "ESV" are from the ESV Bible® (The Holy Bible, English Standard Version®), copyright © 2001 by Crossway Bibles, a publishing ministry of Good News Publishers. Used by permission. All rights reserved.

All Scripture marked with the designation "GW" is taken from GOD'S WORD®. © 1995, 2003, 2013, 2014, 2019, 2020 by God's Word to the Nations Mission Society. Used by permission.

Scripture quotations marked "GNT" are taken from the Good News Translation® (Today's English Version, Second Edition). Copyright © 1992 American Bible Society. All rights reserved. Used by permission.

Scripture quotations marked HCSB are taken from the Holman Christian Standard Bible®, Copyright © 1999, 2000, 2002, 2003 by Holman Bible Publishers. Used by permission. Holman Christian Standard Bible®, Holman CSB®, and HCSB® are federally registered trademarks of Holman Bible Publishers.

Scripture quotations marked "KJV" are taken from the Holy Bible, King James Version (Public Domain).

The Holy Bible, Majority Standard Bible, MSB is produced in cooperation with Bible Hub, Discovery Bible, OpenBible.com, and the Berean Bible Translation Committee. This text of God's Word has been dedicated to the public domain.

Scripture quotations marked "NASB" are taken from the (NASB®) New American Standard Bible®, Copyright © 1960, 1971, 1977, 1995, 2020 by The Lockman Foundation. Used by permission. All rights reserved. lockman.org.

Scripture quoted by permission. Quotations designated (NET) are from the NET Bible® copyright ©1996, 2019 by Biblical Studies Press, L.L.C. http://netbible.com All rights reserved.

Scripture taken from the HOLY BIBLE, NEW INTERNATIONAL VERSION®. NIV®. Copyright © 1973, 1978, 1984 by International Bible Society. Used by permission of Zondervan. All rights reserved worldwide.

Scripture taken from the New King James Version®. Copyright © 1982 by Thomas Nelson. Used by permission. All rights reserved.

Scripture quotations marked NLT are taken from the Holy Bible, New Living Translation, Copyright © 1996, 2004, 2015 by Tyndale House Foundation. Used by permission of Tyndale House Publishers, Inc., Carol Stream, Illinois 60188. All rights reserved.

Scripture quotations marked "NRSV" are taken from the New Revised Standard Version Updated Edition. Copyright © 2021 National Council of Churches of Christ in the United States of America. Used by permission. All rights reserved worldwide.

Scripture quotations marked "NRSV" are taken from the Revised Standard Version of the Bible, copyright © 1946, 1952, and 1971 National Council of the Churches of Christ in the United States of America. Used by permission. All rights reserved worldwide.

Scripture quotations marked TLB are taken from The Living Bible, copyright © 1971 by Tyndale House Foundation. Used by permission of Tyndale House Publishers, Carol Stream, Illinois 60188. All rights reserved.

Scriptures marked WEB are taken from the World English Bible (WEB): World English Bible, public domain.

Disclaimer: Although the author is a licensed mental health professional, all content in this book is for informational purposes only. This publication is not intended to treat, diagnose, or cure any medical or mental health conditions. No parts of this book are to be constituted as medical or mental health advice or to be utilized in lieu of medical or mental health treatment. Results of this written material vary by individual and are not guaranteed.

My Spiritual Growth Journey Begins Today!

_____
Today's Date

"Like newborn infants, desire the pure milk of the word, so that by it you may grow up into your salvation."
-1 Peter 2:2 CSB

"Therefore let us leave the elementary teachings about Christ and go on to maturity, not laying again the foundation of repentance from dead works, and of faith in God."
-Hebrews 6:1 BSB

Table of Contents

Acknowledgments 8
Introduction 9
Preface 13
Step 1 (G) : (Put) God First
    What Does It Mean to Put God First? 14
    God First Challenge Week 1: Discover Your *How* and *Why* to Put God First... 15
    Day 1: How Do I Put God First? Part 1: Giving My Time 16
    Day 2: How Do I Put God First? Part 2: Center of Everything 18
    Day 3: How Do I Put God First? Part 3: Giving My Heart 20
    Day 4: How Do I Put God First? Part 4: Giving My Mind 22
    Day 5: How Do I Put God First? Part 5: Putting the Kingdom First 24
    Day 6: What Happens When I Don't Put God First? 26
    Day 7: The Benefits of Putting God First 28
Step 2 (R) : Repent
    What Does It Mean to Repent? 30
    Repent Challenge Week 2: Define and Seek True Repentance 31
    Day 1: What Is Repentance? Part 1: Changing One's Mind 32
    Day 2: What Is Repentance? Part 2: Feeling Remorse 34
    Day 3: What Is Repentance? Part 3: Turning Around 36
    Day 4: What Does It Mean to Confess My Sins? 38
    Day 5: What Is Baptism, and Do I Need to Be Baptized? 40
    Day 6: What Does It Means to Ask For Forgiveness for My Sins? 42
    Day 7: How Do I Know I Am Forgiven for My Sins? 44
    Repent Challenge Week 3: Discover What Sin Is and Why It's a Big Deal 46
    Day 1: What's the Big Deal About Sin? 47
    Day 2: Breaking Up with Sin Is Hard to Do 49
    Day 3: Sin Has Side-effects: Theft, Death, and Destruction 51
    Day 4: What Are Sins of the Heart? 53
    Day 5: Can Addictions Be Considered Sins? 55
    Day 6: What Are Sexual Sins? 57
    Day 7: Other Sins of Conduct 59
Step 3 (O) : Obey
    What Does It Mean to Obey? 61
    Obey Challenge Week 4: Discover Why You Should Obey God's Will and Word 62
    Day 1: Why Should I Obey What's Written in the Bible? 63
    Day 2: Isn't The Bible Outdated? 65
    Day 3: Can't I Just Do What Feels Right to Me? 67
    Day 4: How Does Obedience Benefit Me? 69
    Day 5: Does the Clay Know More Than the Potter? 71
    Day 6: How Can God Really Relate to Me and Understand How Hard It Is? 73

Table of Contents

Day 7: What If I Don't Obey? 75
Week 5: Discover How to Use Your Armor to Fight 77
Day 1: How Do I Use the Belt of Truth and Sword of the Spirit? 78
Day 2: How Do I Use the Breastplate of Righteousness? 80
Day 3: How Do I Use the Gospel of Peace and Helmet of Salvation? 82
Day 4: How Do I Use the Shield of Faith? 84
Day 5: How Do I Use Prayer as a Weapon? 86
Day 6: Don't Fight Alone 88
Day 7: Fully Suit Up Daily 90

Step 4 (W) Worship
What Is Worship? 92
Worship Challenge Week 6: Discover Your *Why* and *How* to Worship 93
Day 1: Read and Study the Bible 94
Day 2: Sing, Dance, Bow, Shout, and Lift Your Hands 96
Day 3: Worship Through Art, Prayer, and Writing 98
Day 4: Worship Through a Lifestyle of Obedience 100
Day 5: Worship Through Giving 102
Day 6: Heart of Worship 104
Day 7: Don't Forsake the Gathering 106

Step 5 (U) Use Spiritual Gifts
What Does It Mean to Use My Spiritual Gifts? 108
Use Your Gifts Challenge Week 7: Discover Your Purpose and Spiritual Gifts 109
Day 1: What Are Spiritual Gifts, and Do I Have One? 110
Day 2: What's the Purpose of Spiritual Gifts? 112
Day 3: Strengths, Talents, and Skills 114
Day 4: How Do I Use My Gifts, Talents, Strengths, and Skills? 116
Day 5: How Do I Discover My Unique Gifts, Talents, and Strengths? 118
Day 6: What is My Purpose? 120
Day 7: How Will Using My Gifts, Strengths, and Talents Help Me to Grow? 122

Step 6 (P) Prayer
What Is Prayer? 124
Prayer Challenge Week 8: Discover Your *Why* 125
Day 1: Why Should I Pray? Part 1 126
Day 2: Why Should I Pray? Part 2 128
Day 3: Why Should I Pray? Part 3 130
Day 4: What Happens When I Don't Pray? Part 1 132
Day 5: What Happens When I Don't Pray? Part 2 134
Day 6: What Happens When I Don't Pray? Part 3 136
Day 7: How Does Prayer Help Me Grow? 138
Week 9: Discover Your *Who* and *Where* 140
Day 1: Who Can Pray? 141

Table of Contents

Step 6 (P) Prayer Continued

Day 2: Who Do I Pray With? 143
Day 3: Who Do I Pray For? 145
Day 4: Who Do I Pray To? 147
Day 5: Where Can I Pray? 149
Day 6: Where Is God? 151
Day 7: How Do I Create A Prayer Space? 153
Prayer Challenge Week 10: Discover Your 155
Day 1: How Often Should I Pray? 156
Day 2: What If I Only Pray When It's My Last Resort? 158
Day 3: How Can I Find More Time to Pray? Part 1 160
Day 4: How Can I Find More Time to Pray? Part 2 162
Day 5: How Can I Find More Time to Pray? Part 3 164
Day 6: How Can I Find More Time to Pray? Part 4 166
Day 7: How Can I Find More Time to Pray? Part 5 168
Prayer Challenge Week 11: Discover Your *How* 170
Day 1: Is There a Correct Way to Pray? 171
Day 2: Do I Need a Prayer Formula? 173
Day 3: How Do I Use Prayer Formulas? Part 1 175
Day 4: How Do I Use Prayer Formulas? Part 2 177
Day 5: How Long Should I Pray? 179
Day 6: How Do I Use a Prayer Journal? 181
Day 7: Does My Attitude Matter When I Pray? 183
Prayer Challenge Week 12: Discover Your *What* 185
Day 1: What Do I Pray About? 186
(Part 1: Friends, Family, Significant Others, and Leadership)
Day 2: What Do I Pray About? 188
(Part 2: Temptations, Stronghold, and Forgiveness)
Day 3: What Do I Pray About? Part 3: School, Work, and Ambitions 190
Day 4: What Do I Pray About? Part 4: Betrayals and Being Wronged 192
Day 5: What Do I Pray About? Part 5: Finances and Basic Needs 194
Day 6: What Do I Pray About? Part 6: Gratitude 196
Day 7: What Do I Pray About? Part 7: Health and Safety 198
Prayer Challenge Week 13: Pray About Your Mental Health 200
Day 1: Anxiety, Worry, and Fear 201
Day 2: Depression 203
Day 3: Trauma 205
Day 4: Grief 207
Day 5: Life Transitions 209
Day 6: Coping Skills and Self-care 211
Day 7: Anger, Resentment, and Unforgiveness 213
Prayer Challenge Week 14: Discover Your Answered Prayers 215
Day 1: How Does God Answer Prayers? Part 1: Messengers 216
Day 2: How Does God Answer Prayers? Part 2: Dreams 218
Day 3: How Does God Answer Prayers? Part 3: Scripture 220
Day 4: How Does God Answer Prayers? Part 4: Closed Doors 222
Day 5: How Does God Answer Prayers? Part 5: Materialization ... 224
Day 6: What If I Don't Get the Answer I Want? 226
Day 7: Does God Ignore Prayers? 228
Prayer for Continual Spiritual Growth 230

Acknowledgements

I would like to express my gratitude to those who have played a pivotal role in my life and spiritual growth. Thank you to my husband, Demetrius, for his love and constant support of all my goals, dreams, and endeavors. Thank you to my mother, Janie, who introduced me to Christ, as a child, by taking me to Sunday school and church each Sunday. She also gifted me my first Bible, which would become the catalyst for my Bible collection obsession. Thank you to my sister, Donesha, and father, Donald, for their continued encouragement. I am grateful for my aunts Joyce and Doris, who taught Sunday school, and ignited my love for learning the Bible. I would also like to give a special thanks to my former English teacher, Claudia Wehmann, for proofreading this devotional book. She helped to cultivate my passion for writing. Most importantly, I give all praise and honor to my Lord and Savior for blessing me with a platform to present God's Word to His people.

Introduction

Why should I read this book?
Are you spiritually dead, dying, infantile, or stagnant? What is it costing you to stay that way? How much more mentally healthy, whole, grateful, fulfilled, joyful, and impactful could you be if you matured in your faith? Spiritual growth is challenging, yet rewarding, and pivotal to how we interpret our worth, life purpose, circumstances, and God's Word. Do you want to deepen your relationship with God in order to experience Him more intensely and fully? Do you want more peace, joy, and life satisfaction? Do you want to learn more about God, love Him more, communicate with Him more, know Him more intimately, serve His people more effectively, and live a life that pleases Him? All these concepts will be covered in this book, so take the plunge. Whether you have been a Christ follower for years or a newbie, we all have room to grow. Do you want to remain in the same status quo, or are you ready to GROW UP?

What is spiritual growth?
Spiritual growth is the deepening and maturing of your relationship with God through changes in your behavioral patterns, thought process, and emotional responses. It is evidenced by increasing your knowledge and understanding of God, strengthening your faith in God, becoming more like Christ in your character, and frequently communicating with God. Spiritual growth is also evident through authentic repentance, a decrease of sinful actions, obedience to His will and commands, and serving others. As you mature in your Christian journey, there will be an augmentation of your love, appreciation, and admiration for God. Your dependence on God and trust in Him will also be enlarged.

Does spiritual growth really matter?
You can come as you are to God, but He does not intend for you to stay that way. Growth is an expectation of the Christian faith. Jesus expressed frustration with His disciples on several occasions due to the lack of

growth in their faith in Him and knowledge of spiritual matters. Likewise, Paul also reprimanded the Corinthian Christians because they still required "spiritual milk" instead of "solid food" (1 Corinthians 3:1-2 NKJV). That is to say, that these believers were still in spiritual infancy based on their thought patterns, attitudes, and behaviors. In congruency, the writer of Hebrews notes that by that point in time, those believers should have been beyond the need for, and understanding of, elementary principles. They should have matured enough to teach their faith to others, but they were still continually engaging in worldly behaviors (Hebrews 5:12 NIV).

How do I know if I am growing?

One way of tracking your spiritual growth is evaluating where you are now in relation to where you started from. Are you better than you were yesterday, last week, last year, or 5 years ago? How have you improved in implementing the 6 elements of spiritual growth outlined in this book: putting God first, repentance, obedience, worship, using your spiritual gifts, and prayer? Avoid comparing yourself to other Christians because you did not begin at the same starting point, nor did you possess the same tools or life experiences as they did. Christ is the only standard and guidepost that truly matters.

You can also measure your production of what Scripture refers to as the fruits of the Spirit. When we are feeding our spiritual nature more than our sinful nature, here are the results: "But the Holy Spirit produces this kind of fruit in our lives: love, joy, peace, patience, kindness, goodness, faithfulness, gentleness and self-control" (Galatians 5:22-23b NLT). It is easier to display these characteristics when life is going well. However, it is a sign of spiritual growth and maturity when you can continue to possess these traits during difficult times such as death of loved ones, wrongful termination, abuse, betrayal, financial distress, failed endeavors, natural disasters, illness, and other crises.

What is faith?

In Christianity *faith* has a double meaning. Firstly, faith refers to believing in the set of biblical principles that affirms the inerrancy of the Scriptures, the existence and supreme authority of the Holy Trinity, and salvation through the death and resurrection of Jesus Christ. Secondly, faith pertains to the trust that God is in control over all things and that He will intervene with needed and applicable aid. Faith asserts that despite the circumstances, God will transform the perceived negative situation into something that benefits the believer and brings glory to Him. The writer of Hebrews defines faith as the following: "To have faith is to be sure of the things we hope for, to be certain of the things we cannot see" (Hebrews 11:1 GNT). It is then emphasized, "But without faith it is impossible to [walk with God and] please Him, for whoever comes [near] to God must [necessarily] believe that God exists and that He rewards those who [earnestly and diligently] seek Him" (Hebrews 11:6 AMP). To diligently and earnestly seek God means to thoroughly search for Him and to sincerely believe that He will be found. Additionally, the epistle of James warns us, "So faith by itself, if it has no works, is dead" (James 2:17 RSV). When you have genuine faith, then you must act on what you believe to be true. Your faith shapes your character in godliness, which causes you to produce good deeds, promote the truth, and adhere to what God has instructed you to do. Faith is meant to guide the morals, worldview, and actions of God's believers. Our fears, feelings, lies from Satan, and societal pressures must never be allowed to take authority over these matters.

What is The GROW UP Challenge?

The GROW UP Challenge is a 6-step guided journey detailing how to grow spiritually. It is a call to Christians to mature in their faith, or in other words, grow up. GROW UP is an acronym for 6 components of spiritual growth: (Put) God first, Repent, Obey, Worship, Use Spiritual Gifts, and Pray. This adventure includes both a devotional book (The Grow Up Challenge Devotional: A 6-step guide to spiritual growth) and workbook (The GROW UP Challenge Workbook: A 6-step guide to spiritual growth). Every chapter in the devotional book begins with a description of one of the 6 steps of Christian spiritual growth. Within each step, there are weekly challenges that are designed to deepen your relationship with God and strengthen your existing faith. The workbook contains daily writing prompts that correlate to each daily devotion.

It is called a challenge because this is an invitation to take part in a spiritual undertaking and overhaul that will push you beyond your comfort zone. It takes effort to grow. Growing up in your faith is not easy or comfortable but it is necessary to experience God more profoundly. Each weekly challenge contains daily devotional readings, which include prayers, scriptures, and key takeaways (referred to as Seeds to Plant, Water, and Ruminate).

How do I use this book?

The GROW UP Challenge Devotional is intended to be used in conjunction with The GROW UP Challenge Workbook. Each daily devotion has a corresponding set of either growth questions or growth exercises in the workbook. For accuracy purposes, take all the pre-assessments in the workbook prior to beginning the daily devotionals, introductions to each step, and the weekly challenges. After filling out the pre-assessments and scoring sheets, then you can begin reading the first step's description and weekly challenge. Read one devotion each day and complete the accompanying growth questions or exercises located in the workbook. Once all the readings and activities have been completed, take the post-assessments to measure and celebrate all the growth you have experienced over the course of 14 weeks. Lastly, read the closing prayer to provide you with a word of final encouragement as you continue your lifelong pursuit of spiritual growth and fruitfulness.

Preface

About the Author

The GROW UP Challenge was created out the author's desire to help others develop tools to grow closer to God, become passionate about God, live a God-centered life, and to love God more than sin. Many had expressed a longing to know more about God, incorporate God and godly principles into their daily lives, and deepen their relationship with Him. However, there was a lack of resources to implement these concepts in practical ways. Thus, the GROW UP Challenge was developed to aid believers in their understanding of spiritual growth, motivate them to make changes, and to equip them on their journeys.

K. A. Baskin-Springer is dedicated to assisting others in the development of their spiritual growth and emotional wellbeing through her work as a licensed professional clinical counselor, board-certified Christian life coach, and ordained church elder. She also utilizes her degree in biblical studies to spread the gospel and teach God's Word to others. For nearly 20 years, she has been a loving, devoted wife and an empowering mother who inspires those around her with her unwavering zeal for God.

Step 1: (Put) God First

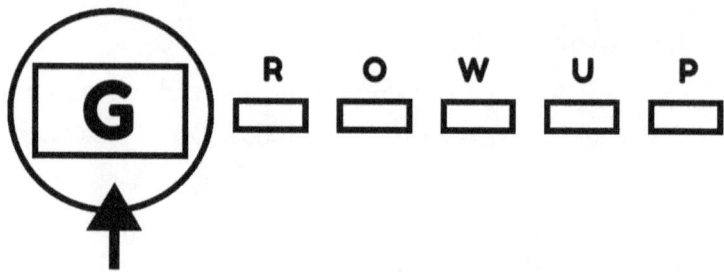

What Does It Mean to Put God First?

Growth Scripture:

"And you shall love the Lord your God with all your heart, and with all your soul, and with all your mind, and with all your strength."
-Mark 12:30 RSV

When we put God first, we are proclaiming that He is important above all else in our lives. God is more significant than our families, friends, careers, money, social media account, country, political party, socioeconomic status, sexual orientation, gender identity, racial identity, drugs, alcohol, clothing, vehicles, sports, food, and societal norms. Our loyalty to God takes precedence over anything and anyone. God's authority is superior to our plans, ambitions, opinions, feelings, rationales, temptations, and desires. He is our priority, and we should elevate His will for our lives above our own. God graciously blesses us with wonderful people, meaningful opportunities, fun entertainment, blissful moments, beautiful places, delicious foods, and valuable possessions; but we must never love these worldly things more than God — our Provider.

God First Challenge: Week 1

Discover Your *Why* and *How* to Put God First

The rationale behind the challenge:

The purpose of this challenge is for you to determine why you will make the life changing commitment to make God your top priority and what that endeavor truly entails. In order to remain dedicated to placing God first in your life, you must wholeheartedly believe that it is to your benefit, crucial to your spiritual growth, and that it is what God requires of you. Once you understand why this concept is so crucial, then you will remain motivated to carry it out despite facing obstacles and opposition. Growth in this area cannot take place without clear steps and objectives. Therefore, this week will detail how to put God first in practical and daily ways.

Growth Quote:

"Then you will call on me and come and pray to me, and I will listen to you. You will seek me and find me when you seek me with all your heart."
-Jeremiah 29.12-13 NIV

Day 1: How Do I Put God First?

Part 1: Giving My Time

Growth Scripture:

"Seek the Lord and his strength; seek his presence continually."
-1 Chronicles 16:11 NRSV

Growth Insight 1: We put God first by giving Him our time. Can we honestly say that some things or individuals are significant to us, yet neglect to invest much time, focus, or energy in them? For example, if I insist that good health is valuable to me, but I do not eat healthily, exercise regularly, rest properly, or manage my stress levels, then my claim appears incongruent with my actions. If you tell a person that he or she is important to you, but you do not call, text, send a letter, visit, talk, provide help, or hang out together, then it is not perceived as very believable or truthful. Likewise, it is necessary to spend ample time engaging in activities such as praying, studying the Bible, reading Christian literature, attending worship services, listening to Christian music, watching godly themed media (i.e., videos, shows, podcasts, prayer apps, movies), and serving others to indicate the significance of God in your life.

Seeds to Plant, Water, and Ruminate:
I need to intentionally prioritize time with God to build my relationship with Him.

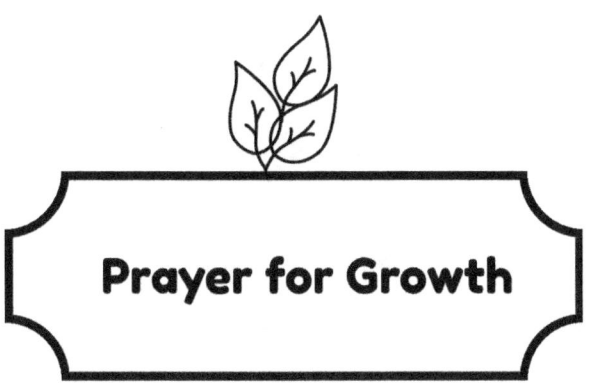

Prayer for Growth

Dear Lord,

You are a priority to me and I want to honor You with my time. It is easy to fill my schedule with all the busy tasks of life and then try to squeeze You in. Lord, please forgive me when I fail to center my day around You, and I leave You out or merely attempt to fit You in. Provide me with wisdom on how I can best prioritize time with You. Help me feel Your presence when I actively seek You.

In Jesus' name, amen.

Day 2: How Do I Put God First?

Part 2: Center of Everything

Growth Scripture:

"In all your ways acknowledge him, and he will make straight your paths."
-Proverbs 3:6 RSV

Growth Insight 2: We put God first by making Him the center of our lives, actions, and decisions. In the late 1990's, there was a cultural phenomenon of books, bracelets, and lessons that encouraged children to ask themselves, "What would Jesus do?" before they acted. Similarly, as adults we should ask ourselves, "Would God approve of this? Will this bring glory and honor to my Heavenly Father? What does the Bible say about this topic? Does this serve myself or God's people? Will this be off-putting to unbelievers or inviting to them?" If God is sincerely the head of our lives, then we do not squeeze Him into our lives and plans or include Him only when it's convenient.

Unlike what the old adage suggests, it is not better to ask for forgiveness than to ask for permission. We need to consult God first and then act. God's Word is the guidepost of every significant decision we make and the measuring stick of right and wrong. It is very tempting to do what we want and justify it later. God has written scripture on our hearts in the form of our conscience. Sometimes we do not want to consult with God first because our conscience is telling us that God does not want this for us. We don't like being accountable to someone else or giving authority to someone else, but we are safe in God's hands. God's life navigational system is better than ours, and His knowledge surpasses our understanding.

Seeds to Plant, Water, and Ruminate:
I have to structure my life around God and His Word. I can't try to fit God into my lifestyle and worldview.

Prayer for Growth

Dear God of the Universe,

Reign over my life. Do with my life as You will and make something beautiful out of the messes I have created. Oh Lord, help me to consult You first before I make decisions. Let Your Word take precedence over my feelings and the influences surrounding me. Send wise, godly people to counsel me and hold me accountable to Your holy scriptures. Thank You for Your aid and constant presence.

In Jesus' name, amen.

Day 3: How Do I Put God First?

Part 3: Giving My Heart

Growth Scriptures:

"As the deer pants for water, so I long for you, O God."
-Psalm 42:1 TLB

"Teach me Your way, O LORD, that I may walk in Your truth. Give me an undivided heart, that I may fear Your name."
-Psalm 86:11 BSB

Growth Insight 3: We put God first by giving Him our hearts. When God has our hearts, we long for Him and we miss His presence when it is not felt. We yearn to feel close to Him and to get to know Him better. When we put God first, we want to hear from Him, we care what He thinks, and we want His approval. If God has our hearts, then we delight in who He is, not just the blessings He provides us with. We marvel at His perfection, omniscience, omnipotence, majesty, kindness, and the complexity of His creation. However, our love for God also produces a sense of gratitude for the nights He comforted us, the sins He has forgiven, the trouble He got us out of, the undeserved grace and mercy He grants to us, the unconditional love He shows us, the guidance He provides, and the things He has healed and delivered us from. The safest place our hearts can be is with our loving Heavenly Father. We can be vulnerable with Him and give Him our complete trust.

Seeds to Plant, Water, and Ruminate:
I long for God and His presence. I delight in Him and His Word.

Prayer for Growth

Dear Magnificent and Eternal Father,

You are wonderful in all of Your ways. Thank You for Your kindness towards me. Thank You for leaving a love letter for me in the form of Your creation and the Bible. I can see the works of Your hands in the stars, in the landscape of the earth, and in the complexities of every organism. Your Word gives me strength, healing, hope, clarity, direction, and peace. Thank You for all You have done for me and my loved ones. Thank You for being there during every high and every low. Help me to fully grasp what it means to love You with all my heart, soul, mind, and strength.

In Jesus' name, I pray. Amen.

Day 4: How Do I Put God First?

Part 4: Giving My Mind

Growth Scripture:

"Do not be conformed to this world, but be transformed by the renewing of your mind. Then you will be able to test and approve what is the good, pleasing, and perfect will of God."
-Romans 12:2 BSB

Growth Insight 4: We put God first by giving Him our mind. In order to keep God first, we have to renew our minds every day with His truth, promises, goodness, and agenda. All day long, we are bombarded with hate, worries, tragic news, temptations, interpersonal conflicts, judgment, belittlement, crime, selfish desires, addictive substances, and even the romanticization of sexual sin and other forms of sin. How can we avoid prioritizing the things of this world and conforming to worldly behavior, if our minds are not fixed on God? The false promises of sin, negativity of society, and busyness of life will overwhelm us unless we give our thoughts to God. We must fill our minds with the Word of God, His lordship and salvation, His will and purpose for us, His kindness towards us, His joy and strength, and the comfort and peace He provides. We must look for the good we see in others and perform acts of love. When we are in love with someone, passionate about something, or trying to accomplish a goal, it's difficult to think about anything else. Then how much more should we think of our Creator, Lord, and Savior?

Seeds to Plant, Water, and Ruminate:
When I focus on God, it keeps everything else in perspective.

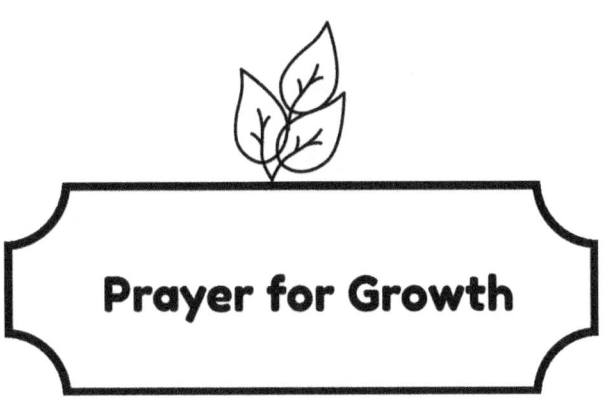

Prayer for Growth

Dear Lord,

I am thankful that You are mindful of me and that You are attentive towards me. You have good thoughts about me and good intentions for me. Help me to keep my mind focused on You daily. I am flooded with distractions, negative influences, and problems all day long. Help me to meditate on Your affirmations, commands, guidance, love, wisdom, peace, capabilities, and goodness throughout the day.

In Jesus' name, amen.

Day 5: How Do I Put God First?

Part 5: Putting the Kingdom First

Growth Scriptures:

"But seek first God's Kingdom and his righteousness; and all these things will be given to you as well."
-Matthew 6:33 WEB

"For what does it profit a man to gain the whole world and to lose his soul?"
-Mark 8:36 BLB

Growth Insight 5: We put God first by putting His kingdom first and giving Him lordship over our desires and actions. Serving God through the service of others, spreading God's message, pleasing Him, and obeying His will and Word is putting His kingdom first. His kingdom refers to the acknowledgement that we are under God's authority and rulership. In the Ten Commandments, God makes it clear that we do not serve any god besides Him and that nothing should be placed above Him. God is aware of our needs and wants. When our desires line up with His Word, will, and timing, God grants us these things liberally.

Furthermore, when accumulating money, pleasing other people, advancing in our careers, having fun, experiencing the effects of drugs or alcohol, choosing our own gender identity or sexual orientation, fornicating, or obtaining power and higher social status is more important than the pursuit of God, then we are not putting His kingdom first. If we are actively compromising our spiritual beliefs to be approved by secular society and to be perceived as tolerant, then God's kingdom is not first in our lives. Jesus states that we are to be light and salt to the world, which will draw people to His kingdom (Matthew 5:13-16). If we lose our unique saltiness, then we negate our kingdom effectiveness.

There may be times when we don't understand how something can be wrong when it feels good or when society says it is right. Just like a parent, God cares about our feelings. Nonetheless, God won't allow our wavering feelings and limited knowledge to dictate His morality. Is gaining the approval of others and indulging in temporary pleasures worth forfeiting your soul and missing out on God's glorious eternal kingdom?

Seeds to Plant, Water, and Ruminate:
I am not the final authority over my life—God is.

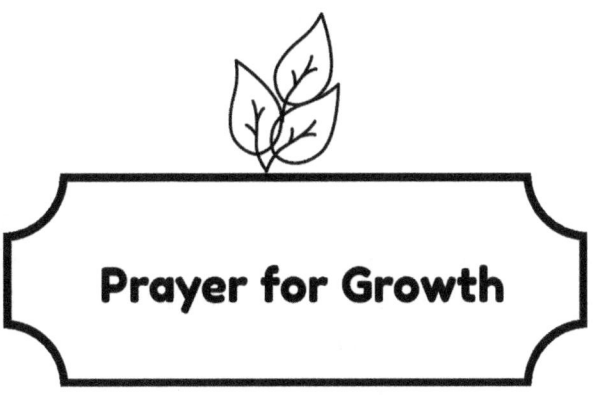

Prayer for Growth

Dear Lord of Angel Armies,

You reign over all the universe. You are the only God and no created being is equivalent to You. You and Your laws are perfect. Thank You for loving me and dying for me when I did not know You or love You. I surrender any desires that I have that are displeasing to You and contrary to Your Word. Honoring You and advancing Your kingdom is more important than conforming to the morals of this world, pleasing others, and satisfying my desires. Help me to trust that Your Word and will is best for me even when I do not understand the reasoning. Guide me away from Satan's traps and from the sinful persuasion from others who are not putting You first.

In Jesus's name, I pray. Amen.

Day 6: What Happens When I Don't Put God First?

Growth Scripture:

"Do not be deceived: God is not to be mocked. Whatever a man sows, he will reap in return. The one who sows to please his flesh, from the flesh will reap destruction; but the one who sows to please the Spirit, from the Spirit will reap eternal life. Let us not grow weary in well-doing, for in due time we will reap a harvest if we do not give up."
-Galatians 6:7-9 BSB

Growth Insight: If you do not put God first in your life, then it is out of order and will not function properly. It is like turning the base of the pyramid on its top and wondering why it is unstable and ultimately falls over. If God is not first, then that means something else is taking God's rightful place and controlling the direction of our minds, passions, ambitions, motives, and actions. God is our guidepost—not our emotional reasoning, not the pressure from our peers, not our careers, not the new social trends, not horoscopes, not social media, not Hollywood, not our social networks, not our fears, and not our mental disorders.

When we put significant others, friends, or family members above God, we are completely devastated and lose direction when they die, abandon us, withhold their love, or disapprove of us. When we put social pressure and progressive morality above what God has commanded of us, then we are displeasing and dishonoring God. When we put irrational thoughts from our trauma, anxiety, depression, delusions, or hallucinations above the truth of God's Word, then we give away and/or do not recognize our power, potential, purpose, and personal worth.

Seeds to Plant, Water, and Ruminate:
I sacrifice intimacy with God, spiritual growth, life fulfillment, and many blessings when I don't put God first.

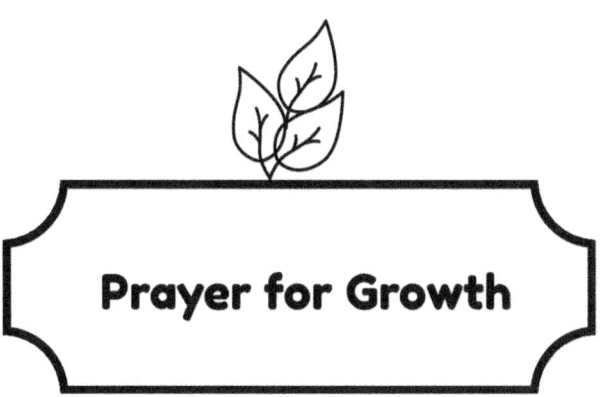

Prayer for Growth

Dear Heavenly Father,

The greatness of Your power, love, mercy, and wisdom, I can never fully comprehend. Please be patient with me as I discover how to keep my heart, soul, mind, and strength focused on You. If there is anything I hold above You in my life, help me to recognize it and prioritize You instead. Empower me to spread Your Word, serve others with love, keep Your commands, and to delight in You.

In Jesus' name, amen.

Day 7: The Benefits of Putting God First

Growth Scriptures:

"We know that all things work together for good for those who love God, for those who are called according to his purpose."
-Romans 8:28 WEB

"The angel of the LORD encamps around those who fear Him [with awe-inspired reverence and worship Him with obedience], And He rescues [each of] them. O taste and see that the LORD [our God] is good; How blessed [fortunate, prosperous, and favored by God] is the man who takes refuge in Him."
-Psalm 34:7-8 AMP

Growth Insight: We don't choose to follow God just to see what we can get out of the deal. We serve God because of who He is. Nevertheless, God is so good that when we put Him first, we do receive many blessings. When God is in His rightful place, we have more peace, clarity, joy, hope, gratitude, and love in our hearts. We gain fulfillment in knowing that we are doing what we were created to do and that it pleases God. God sends us comfort, help, and strength in times of trouble. When we put God first, our suffering is not in vain because all things work together for the good of those who love the Lord. Our worth and capabilities are validated by God. We realize that Christ would have died if it were just us, and no one else. When we put God first, our desires align with His will and Word. As a result, He gifts us with the godly desires of our heart. The more we put God first, the more we look like Christ in our actions. We are set free from sin and from the lies of the Enemy by the truth in His Word.

Seeds to Plant, Water, and Ruminate:
God doesn't instruct me to put Him first for His benefit. Putting God first benefits me and those around me.

Prayer for Growth

Dear Lord,

My Master, I praise Your holy name. I pray that I don't forsake the blessing of keeping You first in my life. You have been faithful to me when I have strayed from You and put my desires, other people, ambitions, sin, opinions of others, and society above You. Please forgive me for my trespasses. You are Lord of my life. I thank You for the blessings I receive when I seek You first and the grace You provide me when I don't.

In Jesus' name, amen.

Step 2: Repent

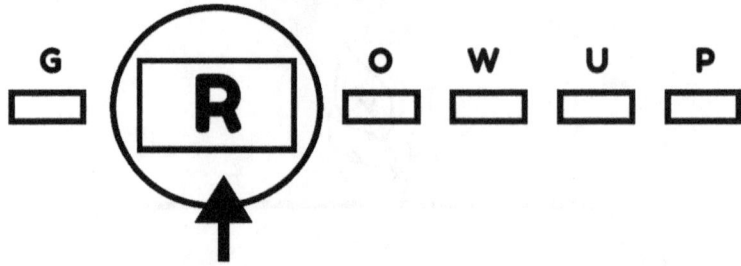

What Does It Mean To Repent?

In both the Old Testament and New Testament, the word *repent* denotes a sense of changing one's mind regarding sin, turning around from the current course, and feeling remorseful. Authentic repentance means that we have turned away from our sin and turned towards God. That is to say, we change the way we think about sin and how we respond to sin. We no longer experience joy while sinning or view it as good or indifferent. When we repent, we not only feel bad about committing the sin, but there is also a change of heart and behavior. As a result, there will be places, people, activities, and items we avoid to no longer put ourselves in a compromising position. During repentance, we acknowledge that our actions are wrong, we feel a sense of conviction, we ask God for forgiveness, we change our desire to sin, and we alter our behavior.

Growth Quote:

"True repentance hates the sin, and not merely the consequence; and it hates the sin most of all because it has discovered and felt God's love."
-William Taylor

Repent Challenge: Week 2

Define and Seek True Repentance

The rationale behind the challenge:

The goal of this challenge is for you to comprehend the necessity of repentance, conceptualize what it means to have a repentant heart and life, and to authentically pursue repentance. In this challenge you will explore areas in which repentance is still needed and how to receive forgiveness from God. During this week, you will begin to uproot sinful thoughts, desires, perspectives, and actions that are stifling your spiritual growth and hindering your relationship with God. Just as a seed is planted and concealed in the depths of the dirt, repentance begins as an inward transformation, which is then evidenced by the outward sprouting of the fruits of the Spirit. Without change, there is no repentance or growth. When you repent, it is impossible to remain the same as you were before you confessed your sins and turned away from them. Repentance is not a one-time act of weeding and pruning sin, but rather a lifelong commitment of spiritual refinement.

Growth Quote:

"If you can sin and not weep over it, you are an heir of Hell. If you can go into sin, and afterwards feel satisfied to have done so, you are on the road to destruction. If there are no prickings of conscience, no inward torments, no bleeding wounds; if you have no throbs and heavings of a bosom that cannot rest; if your soul never feels filled with wormwood and gall when you know you have done evil, you are no child of God."
-Charles Spurgeon

Day 1: What Is Repentance?

Part 1: Changing One's Mind

Growth Scripture:

"Woe unto them that call evil good, and good evil; that put darkness for light, and light for darkness; that put bitter for sweet, and sweet for bitter!"
-Isaiah 5:20 KJV

Growth Insight 1: When we repent from sin, it means that we view sin differently. Our minds are focused on pleasing God with our actions instead of satisfying our selfish desires or gaining the approval of the world. Sin is no longer glorified, guiltlessly desirable, or shamelessly pursued. The thought patterns and behaviors that we once believed were acceptable are now seen in a new light. We realize that our actions have been wrong, and that sin grieves God. We come to understand that God's commands are out of love for His creation and that sin is evil and harms us all. A repentant heart no longer loves sin nor makes excuses for it to continue in one's life. True repentance strives to live righteously and views seeking the pleasures of sin as frivolous and dishonoring to God.

Seeds to Plant, Water, and Ruminate:
I want to view sin as God sees it.

Prayer for Growth

Dear Lord,

You are gracious and holy. Thank You for being patient and merciful towards me. Help me to view sin as You do. I pray that my heart does not become callous towards sin or turn a blind eye to it. Help me to see the graveness of my sins and not justify them in my own mind. Lord, help me to seek and love Your truth and be grieved by what grieves You. Strengthen me to help guide, correct, love, and encourage my brothers and sisters, in Christ, as they struggle with sin.

In Jesus' name, amen.

Day 2: What Is Repentance?

Part 2: Feeling Remorse

Growth Scripture:

"Godly sorrow brings repentance that leads to salvation and leaves no regret, but worldly sorrow brings death."
- 2 Corinthians 7:10 NIV

Growth Insight 2: Remorse is a good thing. Any sin in our lives should greatly trouble us. There is a sense of remorse, guilt, and distress when we genuinely have a repentant heart. We are sorrowful for sinning against our Creator, Provider, Healer, Protector, Comforter, Savior, and Lord. We should not choose to ignore our sin, become desensitized to it, love it, be indifferent towards it, or be flippant about it. True repentance does not resent God or have anger towards Him for establishing and enforcing His commands. A person with a repentant heart feels sorrowful and regrets sin, which becomes the catalyst to turn away from it and sin no more.

Seeds to Plant, Water, and Ruminate:
Remorse is not meant to leave me immobilized in self-demoralization. It is present to deter me from continuing down a sinful path. Remorse is a symptom of my sinful nature at battle with my spiritual self.

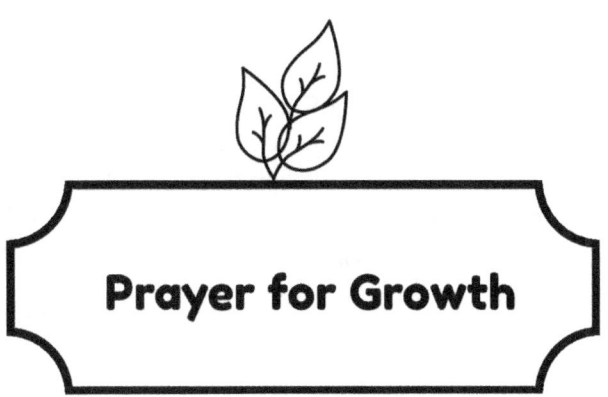

Prayer for Growth

Dear Heavenly Father,

Thank You for Your compassion and love for me. Lord, You have written Your laws on my heart, which convicts me when I am at fault. Help my empathy to dissuade me from doing wrong to others and my love for You to keep me from sinning against You. Allow remorse to prevent me from loving sin and continuing to sin. Please do not allow my remorse to leave me in a prolonged state of shame and despair. Contrarily, help my remorse to lead me to repentance and to seek Your forgiveness.

In Jesus' name, amen.

Day 3: What Is Repentance?

Part 3: Turning Around

Growth Scriptures:

"No one who abides in Him [who remains united in fellowship with Him—deliberately, knowingly, and habitually] practices sin. No one who habitually sins has seen Him or known Him."
-1 John 3:6 AMP

"Whoever is a believer in Christ is a new creation. The old way of living has disappeared. A new way of living has come into existence."
-2 Corinthians 5:17 GW

Growth Insight 3: During repentance we take a different life direction. We are no longer on the wrong path, which leads to death. We are pursuing God instead of chasing after sin. True repentance means that we no longer live the same sinful lifestyle as before. In essence, we turn our backs to sin and walk towards God. We follow God's guidance and leave our own rationalizations and evil desires behind. Without change there is no true repentance.

Seeds to Plant, Water, and Ruminate:
I cannot live the way I used to live. A change of heart must lead to a change in my conduct.

Prayer for Growth

Dear Lord,

You reign over heaven and earth. I pray that You also reign over my heart, spirit, beliefs, priorities, thoughts, and actions. Please turn my heart from sin so that I do not continue the sins in which I have been engaging. Strengthen me to resist temptation and to seek you when I am in need of help. Help me to realize that even if I have an intermittent sin, I am not a slave to habitual sin. Thank You for Your power that can break any stronghold and that strengthens me when I feel weak, helpless, and hopeless.

I pray these things in Jesus' name, amen.

Day 4: What Does It Mean to Confess My Sins?

Growth Scripture:

"If we say that we have no sin, we deceive ourselves, and the truth is not in us. If we confess our sins, he is faithful and just to forgive us our sins, and to cleanse us from all unrighteousness."
-1 John 1:8-9 KJV

Growth Insight: Confessing your sins means that you have admitted the wrongdoings that you have committed against God and others. Confession also includes taking full responsibility for your actions—not shifting the blame and not making excuses. Confession of your sins is one of the preconditions of salvation. You must acknowledge that you need a savior and know why you need one in the first place. Confession is a result of your genuine conviction about sin; it is not to be done out of coercion or mere ritual.

Seeds to Plant, Water, and Ruminate:
When I confess my sins, I acknowledge that there is a moral lawgiver, that I'm under His authority, and that I am in violation.

Prayer for Growth

Dear Lord,

You are the Most High God and Ruler of the Universe. I come before You with all humility, reverence, and honesty. Please help me to recognize the sins I have committed. There are some sins that I struggle to understand why they are wicked and offensive to You. Allow me to view these sins from Your perspective. Remind me that Your knowledge and wisdom exceed my own. You are the Potter, and I am the clay. Help me to realize that Your commands are always for my benefit. You are not a malicious, tyrannical, arbitrary, or self-serving God. Thank You for Your grace and mercy.

In Jesus' name, amen.

Day 5: What Is Baptism, and Do I Need to Be Baptized?

Growth Scriptures:

"Then Peter said unto them, Repent, and be baptized every one of you in the name of Jesus Christ for the remission of sins, and ye shall receive the gift of the Holy Ghost."
-Acts 2:38 KJV

"Go ye therefore, and make disciples of all the nations, baptizing them into the name of the Father and of the Son and of the Holy Spirit."
-Matthew 28:19 ASV

Growth Insight: Immersion into the water is an outward expression of an inward faith that Christ is Savior. It is symbolic of dying to sin, being buried with Christ, and rising as a new and cleansed creation (Romans 6:4). However, there is no unanimous consensus in the Christian faith regarding whether or not baptism is a requirement for salvation. Some differing opinions, regarding baptism, stem from the fact that the saints of the Old Testament were saved through their faith. Additionally, the thief on the cross wasn't dipped in the water when Jesus said He'll see him that night in paradise. Others argue that requiring baptism for salvation would be insinuating a works-based salvation, which is unbiblical. Luke recounts that Peter instructed others to be baptized for the remission of sins (Acts 2:38). Most importantly, Jesus tells Nicodemus that unless one is born again, with water and spirit, then that person will not see the kingdom of heaven (John 3:5). Moreover, it is clear that Jesus commands believers to be baptized (Matthew 28:19). Thus, if Jesus said it, then we should do it.

Seeds to Plant, Water, and Ruminate:
Baptism is a physical representation of the cleansing from sins that I have already received.

Prayer for Growth

Dear Lord,

Thank You for Your saving grace. Thank you for cleansing my sins through the blood of Christ's sacrifice. I'm so grateful that Jesus took my place and paid my debt. Thank You for the gift of baptism, which enables me to symbolically share in Christ's death, burial, and resurrection. Aid me in feeling closer to You and conceptualizing the reality of my salvation through the experience of baptism.

In Jesus' name, amen.

Day 6: What Does It Means to Ask for Forgiveness for My Sins?

Growth Scripture:

"Have mercy on me, O God, because of your unfailing love. Because of your great compassion, blot out the stain of my sins. Wash me clean from my guilt. Purify me from my sin. For I recognize my rebellion; it haunts me day and night. Against you, and you alone, have I sinned; I have done what is evil in your sight."
-Psalm 51:1-4b NLT

Growth Insight: We have all sinned by disobeying God's commandments. Our nature and bodies have been corrupted by sin. As a result of breaking God's laws, we have been physically and spiritually separated from Him, and the penalty is death. God is just so there has to be a penalty for all the harm and evil committed in the world. However, God is also gracious and merciful. Jesus died on the cross to absolve those individuals who have asked for forgiveness and accepted Christ as their Lord and Savior. Those individuals will not experience an eternal suffering or separation from God. In order to be forgiven, you must follow these four steps. 1. Believe you have sinned and confess your sins to God. 2. Believe He has the power and authority to save you from eternal damnation. 3. Believe that Jesus took your penalty and paid your debt for sin. 4. Ask to be forgiven for all of the offenses you have committed.

Seeds to Plant, Water, and Ruminate:
Jesus loves me so much that He came to Earth, was beaten, disrespected, spit on, cursed, nailed to a cross, and killed to pay my debt.

Prayer for Growth

Dear Heavenly Father,

You reign supreme over all of of creation. You are Judge over all but have also provided a Savior. Lord, I have sinned against you by breaking Your laws. Please forgive me for the sins I have committed, those known and unknown, past and future. Please forgive me for the pain I have caused You and others. Thank You for Jesus' suffering and dying on the cross to take away my guilt and to pay my debt to You. Thank You for sending the Holy Spirit to guide me and empower me.

In Jesus' name, amen.

Day 7: How Do I Know I Am Forgiven for My Sins?

Growth Scripture:

"Because if you acknowledge and confess with your mouth that Jesus is Lord [recognizing His power, authority, and majesty as God], and believe in your heart that God raised Him from the dead, you will be saved. For with the heart a person believes [in Christ as Savior] resulting in his justification [that is, being made righteous—being freed of the guilt of sin and made acceptable to God]; and with the mouth he acknowledges and confesses [his faith openly], resulting in and confirming [his] salvation."
-Romans 10:9-10 AMP

Growth Insight:
Step 1: Believe that Jesus is Lord and has authority to forgive sins.
Step 2: Believe you have sinned and are in need of a savior.
Step 3: Believe that Jesus died for the forgiveness of your sins.
Step 4: Repent by turning your heart and actions away from sin.
Step 5: Confess your sins to God.
Step 6: Ask God to forgive you of your sins.
Step 7: Be baptized.
Step 8: Believe that you have been forgiven.

Faith is a huge part of salvation. You have to believe that what God said is true, that it applies to you, and that it never changes. Have confidence that if you have completed these steps, then you are saved from God's judgment and have been forgiven of your sins. Once you have accepted Jesus as your Lord and Savior, you cannot be snatched away from His eternal grace and deliverance. Praise God!

Seeds to Plant, Water, and Ruminate:
I don't have to do anything to earn salvation. I am saved by my faith that Jesus is Lord and that He has forgiven my sins.

Prayer for Growth

Dear God of Grace and Mercy,

Thank You for loving me despite my rebellion against You. Thank You for forgiving my sins. Help me to not return to my old ways. Lord, I want to serve you and seek Your will for my life. Help me to love You with all of my heart, soul, mind, and strength. Lord, help me to love You more than any sin. Please strengthen my faith in You and settle any doubts that I may have. Thank You for encasing my life with Your grace and mercy.

In Jesus' name, I pray. Amen.

Repent Challenge: Week 3

Discover What Sin Is and Why It's a Big Deal

The rationale behind the challenge:

In order to better understand the meaning and significant of repentance, you must first comprehend what you are repenting from: sin. Sin is any offense against God, an act of rebellion against God, or a violation of His commands. Sin is also frequently referenced as disobedience to God or being evil. It can further be explained as a wrongdoing or a missing of the mark of righteousness. Sin separates us physically and spiritually from God, which is why we need salvation in order to be reconciled with Him. Sin hurts us and the others around us. Our sinful nature goes against God's will, intent, and design for our lives.

Growth Scripture and Growth Quote:

"But each person is tempted when he is drawn away and enticed by his own evil desires. Then after desire has conceived, it gives birth to sin, and when sin is fully grown, it gives birth to death."
-James 1:14-15 HCSB

"Hell is the highest reward that the devil can offer you for being a servant of his."
-Billy Sunday

Day 1: What's the Big Deal About Sin?

Growth Scripture:

"For the wages of sin is death; but the free gift of God is eternal life in Christ Jesus our Lord."
-Romans 6:23 ASV

Growth Insight: We've all heard of white lies, victimless crimes, and doing what you want to as long as it doesn't affect someone else. These concepts are false and misleading. Sin always affects someone else: God and your relationship to Him. Some people view sin as harmless or argue that it is subjective. Contrarily, sin is not subjective. God is the Lawgiver and defines morality, not us. Sin separates us from God and is worthy of physical and spiritual death. Sin is serious! Don't let anyone convince you that sin is no big deal or that it is excusable because "everyone does it." Your sin is not voided because others have sinned as well. Our Lord will judge every person based on his or her own actions. Even if you sin with so-called *good intentions*, fail to understand why it's wrong, or choose to not accept its sinfulness, it's still evil in God's eyes.

Seeds to Plant, Water, and Ruminate:
Sin is so serious that Jesus had to leave His throne in heaven and come to Earth to die for my sins or else I would be separated from God eternally.

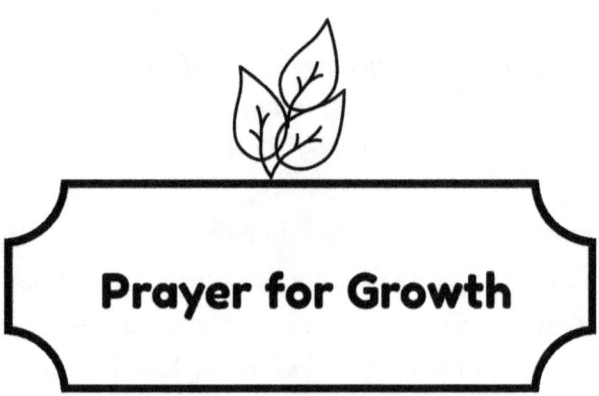

Prayer for Growth

Dear God,

I thank You for being patient with me, showing me mercy, and offering Your grace. Thank You for Your gift of salvation and Jesus' sacrifice on the cross. Open my eyes to view sin as You do. Consume my thoughts so that I do not fail to consider whether or not my intentions and plans are pleasing to You before I act. Help me to never become complacent with my sin or to make excuses for it. Make me aware of how my sins have grieved You and caused suffering. Give me the courage to own up to my sins and strive to change. Grant me with the strength and knowledge of Your Word that I need to resist temptation.

In Jesus' name, amen.

Day 2: Breaking Up with Sin Is Hard to Do

Growth Scriptures:

"The temptations in your life are no different from what others experience. And God is faithful. He will not allow the temptation to be more than you can stand. When you are tempted, he will show you a way out so that you can endure."
-1 Corinthians 10:13 NLT

"But he said to me, "My grace is enough for you, for my power is made perfect in weakness." So then, I will boast most gladly about my weaknesses, so that the power of Christ may reside in me."
-2 Corinthians 12:9 NET

Growth Insight: Repentance is not an easy thing to accomplish or maintain. We must ask for God's help to change our hearts and to give us strength to resist temptation. Scripture tells us that God always gives us a way out of temptation, and that we are not tempted beyond what we can endure or overcome. Sometimes we see the out and do not take it; other times, we refuse to see. However, He is merciful, and we do not have to go at it alone. God is always there to help you. When you are weak, you can lean on God's strength. You can also seek out mature and confidential Christians to help encourage you, pray for you, and hold you accountable. Church small groups, support groups, coaching, therapy, and self-help books are great options as well.

Seeds to Plant, Water, and Ruminate:
God wants me to come to Him with my weaknesses. Being too proud to ask for His help keeps me enslaved to my sin.

Prayer for Growth

Dear Lord,

You are my constant help, hope, and strength. Sometimes I feel alone in my situation, but I know You are always there for me and with me. There are days that I feel like a bad Christian and that I'll never get it right. I sometimes hide from You, and those who want to help me, out of shame that I am still struggling with the same issues. There are some sins I struggle to give up out of fear of having nothing to fill the void. Help to remind me that You are enough for me. If I have You, then I have all that I need. Help me to understand that no Christian is perfect, but I should continue to strive to be like Christ. What You have for me is better than what sin can offer me. Please forgive me of my sins. Provide me with a clear way out, the tools I need, and the wisdom to use them.

In Jesus' name, I pray. Amen.

Day 3: Sin Has Side-effects: Theft, Death, and Destruction

Growth Scripture:

"The thief comes only to steal and kill and destroy. I came that they may have life, and have it abundantly."
-John 10:10 NRSV

Growth Insight: Satan and his demons do not have your best interest in mind. When he tempts you with anything God has prohibited, it is not intended to be harmless. Having fun, experiencing pleasure, and living your so-called *truth* or *best life*, is not the Enemy's end goal. Sin maybe laid before you in an alluring trail of gold nuggets. However, closer examination reveals that its shinny exterior is merely fool's gold. Sin is worthless but comes with a hefty price. Once you embrace the fool's gold, you also discover that you're caught in a trap, enslaved to sin and addictions. Satan's plan is to steal your sense of purpose, salvation, peace, joy, hope, worth, and identity. The Enemy is not satisfied with merely getting you fired due to stealing, leaving you homeless because of gambling debts, depriving you of sexual intimacy (in marriage) due to pornography addiction, leaving you insecure and unfilled in cohabitation, getting you strung out on drugs, distorting your gender identity and sexual orientation, destroying your marriage by adultery, or incarcerating you for fraudulent crimes. He wants to kill you! That is, kill your faith, willpower, mind, body, and soul/spirit.

Seeds to Plant, Water, and Ruminate:
Despite what society promotes or portrays, sin does not help me live my best life.

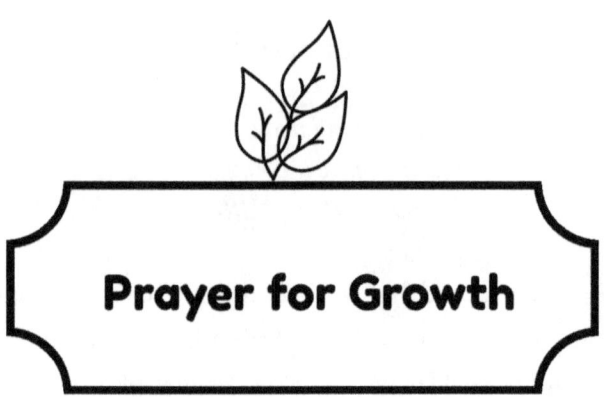

Prayer for Growth

Dear God of Truth,

Please expose the tricks, snares, and lies of the Enemy. Help me to not be lured away by the false promises of sin or lead others astray. Remind me that sin results in emptiness, theft, death, and destruction. Let me seek to please You in all that I do instead of trying to find a loophole to excuse sinful behaviors. Lord, please remind me that following You leads me to my best life. Learning Your truth and abiding by it, frees me from lies and bondage. Thank You for the liberty and nourishment that I receive from Your Word.

I pray these things in Jesus' name, amen.

Day 4: What Are Sins of the Heart?

Growth Scriptures:

"Search me, O God, and know my heart: try me, and know my thoughts: And see if there be any wicked way in me, and lead me in the way everlasting."
-Psalm 139:23-24 KJV

"Above all else, guard your heart, for everything you do flows from it."
-Proverbs 4:23 NIV

Growth Insight: Sins of the heart deal with our attitude, thoughts and our feelings towards people, things, and situations. Examples of sins of the heart are as follows: envy, pridefulness, arrogance, condescendence, ungodly wrath, unforgiveness, greed, hatred, racism, vengefulness, selfishness, and lack of faith (i.e. in God). We are commanded to love one another regardless of race, socioeconomic status (poor, rich, slave, free, government official, civilian, etc.), gender, sexual orientation, nationality, kinship, or age. We are also commanded to give generously and to forgive our enemies and others. God requires that we have faith in Him and that we forgive those who have wronged us. Scripture warns us to not think too highly of ourselves and to not boast in front of others. This does not mean that we should have low self-esteem, but we should be humble and remember that who and what we are is due to God's grace and mercy. Lastly, we are to be grateful for what God has given us and not resentfully covet what God has given others. The Bible says that God examines our hearts. Therefore, our motives and beliefs matter to Him as much as our actions.

Seeds to Plant, Water, and Ruminate:
God examines my heart because it is a reflection of my thoughts, loyalties, motives, and actions.

Prayer for Growth

Dear God,

My Master, my heart belongs to You. Please purify my heart and remove any hatred, envy, pride, vengeance, racism, greed, selfishness, unforgiveness, or doubt that may exist within me. Help me to comprehend that these things are self-destructive and tears down those around me. Help me to build others up and to have a heart of humility and gratitude. Sins of the heart also get in the way of my relationship with You and impedes my blessings. Thank You for Your righteousness and faithfulness.

In Jesus' name, amen.

Day 5: Can Addictions Be Considered Sins?

Growth Scriptures:

"No one can serve two masters, for either he will hate the one and love the other, or he will be devoted to the one and despise the other. You cannot serve God and money."
-Matthew 6:24 ESV

"Be sober-minded; be watchful. Your adversary the devil prowls around like a roaring lion, seeking someone to devour."
-1 Peter 5:8 ESV

Growth Insight: When we become addicted to anything, then it is not God who we live to serve, please, and worship. The addiction becomes a false god that we must obey and do unseemly things to satisfy. The addiction is our first priority and not God. The problem is that we cannot put anything in God's place and expect to be blessed, function at our best, and avoid causing damage to ourselves and others. When we are under the influence of something else, we cannot be under God's influence at the same time. Addictions are not just restricted to drugs (prescription or illicit) and alcohol; they can also include things such as gambling, gaming, fantasy, gluttony, sex, pornography, caffeine, smoking, the accumulation of wealth, and so on. You cannot serve both God and your addiction. If you are struggling with an addiction don't be ashamed to ask for God's help and forgiveness, or to seek help from a therapist, support group, church, doctor, or accountability partner. Just because you've struggled with this addiction for a long time doesn't mean you have to be enslaved to it forever. Where your willpower ends, God's mercy and power begin.

Seeds to Plant, Water, and Ruminate:
I need to be free of addiction in order to be fully receptive to God's truth, be present for my loved ones, function at my best, do God's will, and to resist Satan's lies and temptation.

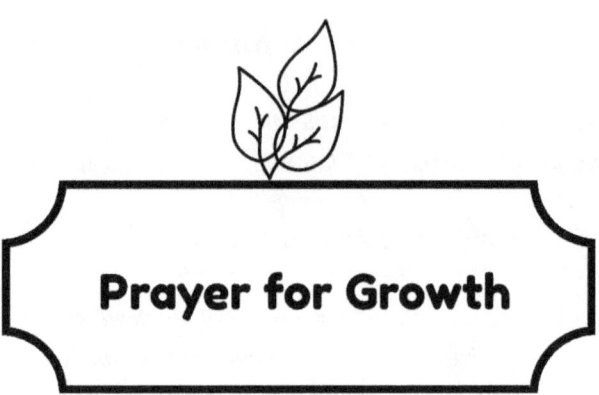

Prayer for Growth

Dear God,

My Healer, I give my addiction over to You. I have relied on my own willpower for so long and it has not worked. Sometimes I feel ashamed that I am struggling with this issue after all this time. My addiction feels hopeless, but I know You are a way maker and my hope. Please remove my desire, fear, and dependency that keeps me trapped in the cycle of self-destruction. I feel so weak, but I know that You are my strength. Lord, thank You for Your unconditional love for me. Thank You for Your patience with me and for Your grace and mercy. Please forgive me for the sins I have committed to feed my addiction.

In Jesus' name, amen.

Day 6: What Are Sexual Sins?

Growth Scriptures:

"Do you not know that the unrighteous will not inherit the kingdom of God? Do not be deceived! The sexually immoral, idolaters, adulterers, passive homosexual partners, practicing homosexuals...will not inherit the kingdom of God."
-1 Corinthians 6:9-10 NET

"God's will is for you to be holy, so stay away from all sexual sin."
-1 Thessalonians 4:3 NLT

Growth Insight: Sexual sins are any behaviors or ruminating thoughts that contain intent to act, pertain to sexuality, and that are against God's commands and will for our lives. God has designed us and is the creator of our sexuality. Therefore, we must trust that He knows what is best for our lives, bodies, minds, and spirits. Even if we do not understand the rationale for each command, we should still adhere to our God's instructions. Jesus states lusting after a person other than your spouse is as serious as and sinful as adultery. Fornication, orgies, and homosexual acts are condemned in the Old Testament laws and in the New Testament letters. Cross-dressing and prostitution are also noted as sin in the Old Testament. God clearly states that He "hates" divorce and Paul states that remarrying while one's former spouse is still alive is considered adultery. Rape, incest, and molestation are also denounced and forbidden throughout the Bible. Scripture states that our bodies are temples, a dwelling place for the Holy Spirit, and should be kept pure and holy.

Seeds to Plant, Water, and Ruminate:
God intended for sexual intimacy to only be shared between husband and wife for the rest of their lives. Sex in any other context is sinful and out of order.

Prayer for Growth

God of Heaven and Earth,

Praise be to Your holy and magnificent name. Thank You for Your wisdom and discernment. Thank You for Your perfect design for marriage, gender, and sexual intimacy. Help me look to You for the ultimate authority on sexual matters and not the world's standards or to myself. Help me to understand the joy, satisfaction, peace, and blessings your design brings. Likewise, open my eyes to the pain, destruction, harm, and confusion that my sins cause me, other individuals, and families. Help me to keep my mind and body holy.

In Jesus' name, amen.

Day 7: Other Sins of Conduct

Growth Scriptures:

"Their lives are filled with all kinds of sexual sins, wickedness, and greed. They are mean. They are filled with envy, murder, quarreling, deceit, and viciousness. They are gossips, slanderers, haters of God, haughty, arrogant, and boastful. They think up new ways to be cruel. They don't obey their parents."
-Romans 1:29-30 GW

"You must never sacrifice your sons or daughters by burning them alive, practice black magic, be a fortuneteller, witch, or sorcerer, cast spells, ask ghosts or spirits for help, or consult the dead."
-Deuteronomy 18:10-11 GW

Growth Insight: Conduct sins are those transgressions that are composed of our outward behaviors. Sins such as stealing, lying, murder, human sacrifice, swindling, cursing others, gossip, dishonoring one's parents, violence, obscene language, and coarse joking are sins that are damaging to the others around us. Whether the impact is immense or minor, it doesn't change its sinfulness. When we practice empathy and consider how we would feel if someone committed these acts towards us, or our loved ones, then it should act as a deterrent. We are commanded to do unto others as we would have them do unto us, and to love our neighbor as ourselves. Contacting the dead (e.g., necromancy, spiritism, séance), fortune telling (e.g., palm readings, tarot cards, horoscopes), witchcraft (e.g., black magic, sorcery), worshipping idols and false gods, and taking the Lord's name in vain are sins against God's sovereignty and discretion. God is Lord over tomorrow, and He reveals what He wants us to know about our future. He is Lord over all and will not accept second place, nor does He deserve it.

Seeds to Plant, Water, and Ruminate:
I trust God with my future and serve no other God but Him. I need to consider how my behavior is viewed by God and impacts others before I act.

Prayer for Growth

Dear Lord,

I want my actions to please You and to reflect my love for You. Please turn my heart away from any sins I struggle with from today's reading. Help me to understand why these things are harmful and against Your will. Help me to trust You and to not consult any mediums, witches, or those who practice divination. Lord, fill the void in my heart that these sins falsely promise to satisfy. Help me to consider the feelings of others before I act. Thank You for Your power, strength, help, guidance, refuge, and constant presence in my life.

In Jesus' name, amen.

Step 3: Obey

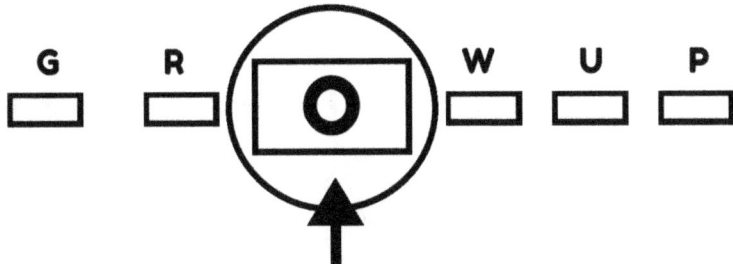

What Does It Mean To Obey?

Obey means that we adhere to God's commands and apply the moral principles of the Bible to our daily lives. The teachings in the Bible dictate our decision making and our actions. We do the things we were charged to do and avoid the sinful things we were instructed not to engage in. Obedience requires that we acknowledge God's authority over our lives, and we carry out His will for us. When we obey God by loving our neighbors, then we'll do things that are for their benefit and not their detriment. For example, telling the truth, showing kindness and mercy, being non-violent, giving generously, not stealing, being patient, remaining faithful in marriage, feeding the hungry, clothing the poor, forgiving others, returning what was borrowed, not provoking or encouraging others to sin, teaching God's Word, praying for others, being respectful, creating peace, helping others to complete tasks, and serving others is loving. When we obey, we are worshipping only one God, seeking righteousness, listening to God's voice, and giving our heart to Him.

Growth Scripture and Growth Quote:

"With all my heart I seek you. Do not allow me to stray from your commands."
-Psalm 119:10 NET

"Grant me, O Lord my God, a mind to know you, a heart to seek you, wisdom to find you, conduct pleasing to you, faithful perseverance in waiting for you, and a hope of finally embracing you. Amen."
-Thomas Aquinas

Obey Challenge: Week 4

Discover Why You Should Obey God's Will and Word

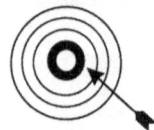

The rationale behind the challenge:

The objective of this week's challenge is for you to obtain an understanding of why it is essential, required, and in your best interest to be obedient to God. It makes it easier to be committed and compliant with God's will and Word when we have an understanding of why we are doing it. Obedience is more palatable, meaningful, impactful, and rewarding when we put it in its proper perspective. Understanding the reasoning of obedience brings you one step closer to spiritual maturation and closeness with God.

Growth Scripture:

"This is the end of the matter; all hath been heard: Fear God, and keep his commandments; for this is the whole duty of man. For God will bring every work into judgment, with every hidden thing, whether it be good, or whether it be evil."
-Ecclesiastes 12:13-14 ASV

Day 1: Why Should I Obey What's Written in the Bible?

Growth Scriptures:

"If you love me, you will obey my commandments."
-John 14:15 GW

"Not everyone who says to me, 'Lord, Lord,' will enter the kingdom of heaven, but only the one who does the will of my Father in heaven."
-Matthew 7:21 NAB

Growth Insight: As children, many of us questioned our parents' motives regarding why they wanted us to comply with certain tasks, rituals, or rules. They could have explained that it was for our own protection, to teach us responsibility, to foster personal growth, to develop our empathy for others, or because they loved us. However, there are some concepts that we can't comprehend at the time so it's easier to just say, "Because I said so."

Jesus makes it clear; if you love Him, then you will obey His commands. It is simple. Do it because He says so! Jesus also emphasizes the point in this verse, "Why do you call me 'Lord, Lord' and do not do what I say?" (Luke 6:46 NASB). If you do not obey, then you do not recognize His authority as your Lord and Savior. You demonstrate your love for God by doing what He says. Following the commandments of the Bible is essential because they are God's words. They are not merely contrived from mankind.

As our relationship with God deepens, we obey the Scriptures because we have become more like Christ, and we want to please Him. Our perspective on life and God's love, wisdom, greatness, and mercy has changed. We obey Him because our actions are now reflecting the internal change that occurs when we allow God to work on our hearts. What was once mere duty or compliance has now become our nature and delight. Remember, Scripture urges us to, "Be doers of the word, and not hearers only. Otherwise, you are deceiving yourselves" (James 1:22 MSB).

Seeds to Plant, Water, and Ruminate:
I obey because I love Him, respect His authority, and am grateful for Christ's sacrifice.

Prayer for Growth

Dear God,

I love You and I want to demonstrate that love for You through my actions. Help me to serve others and treat them the way I would want to be treated. Use me as an instrument to share Your love and Your message through my deeds and words. Guide me as I endeavor to respect Your authority as Lord by obeying Your Word and following Your calling for my life.

In Jesus' name, amen.

Day 2: Isn't The Bible Outdated?

Grow Scriptures:

"Every Scripture passage is inspired by God. All of them are useful for teaching, pointing out errors, correcting people, and training them for a life that has God's approval."
-2 Timothy 3:16 GW

"The grass withers, the flower fades, but the word of our God stands forever."
-Isaiah 40:8 NASB

Growth Insight: It's true that the last book of the Bible was written approximately 2,000 years ago in the ancient Near East (modern day Middle East). However, that doesn't diminish its relevancy for us today. Just because societal norms change as rapidly as the wind, does not mean that cultural times invalidate God's instructions and morality in the scriptures. Paul informs us that all Scripture is useful to teach, rebuke, correct, and to train in righteous living. Isaiah reminds us that the Word of God lasts forever. Solomon proclaims that there is nothing new under the sun (Ecclesiastes 1:9). The writer of Hebrews declares that Jesus is the same yesterday, today, and forever (Hebrews 13:8).

Although the Bible is not a book containing an exhaustive collection of instructions for all life topics, the moral golden thread seen throughout the scriptures can shed light on unwritten subject matters. Nonetheless, there are some Old Testament laws that were specific to Israel's government structure, temple rituals, and animal sacrifices that would not be applicable for several reasons. First, we are instructed to abide by the laws of the land. Second, the temple is no longer needed and doesn't exist. Third, Jesus' death on the cross and New Covenant replaced the sacrificial system. Moreover, Jesus and the New Testament writers reiterate that we are still bound by the Old Testament moral laws in this New Covenant era.

Seeds to Plant, Water, and Ruminate:
God's Word is timeless, relevant, powerful, active, binding, righteous, sacred, and liberating.

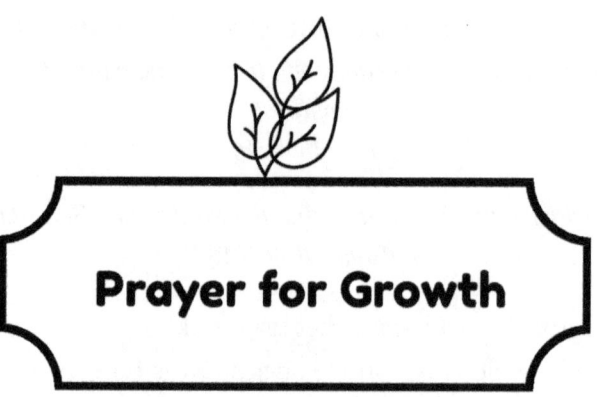

Prayer for Growth

Dear Lord,

Thank You for Your faithfulness to Your Word and to me. Help me to not be swayed or led astray by the subjective ethics of the world. Your Scripture is timeless, just, and righteous. Lord, I want to please You above anyone one else. Help me to discern how to apply Your Word to my life. Help me to be bold and stand by Your Word although society may view biblical morality as outdated or subjective.

In Jesus' name, amen.

Day 3: Can't I Just Do What Feels Right to Me?

Growth Scriptures:

"For from within, out of people's hearts, comes evil thoughts, sexual immoralities, thefts, murders, adulteries, greed, evil actions, deceit, promiscuity, stinginess, blasphemy, pride, and foolishness."
-Mark 7:21-22 HCSB

"There is a path before each person that seems right, but it ends in death"
-Proverbs 14:12 NLT

"The heart is deceitful above all things And it is extremely sick; Who can understand it fully and know its secret motives?"
-Jeremiah 17:9 AMP

Growth Insight: Have you heard phrases like, "My intentions were good," "How can it be wrong if it feels so right?" "The end justifies the means," or "How can it be wrong when it seems to make them happy?" It is inadvisable to solely base your morality, decisions, and actions on the whims of your own reasoning, feelings, or societal norms. Jeremiah informs us that our hearts can deceive us because they are sick and corrupted. Jesus expands upon this concept by giving many examples of what sinful things come from the heart. Our actions are a reflection of what is already in our hearts. Thus, we need God to cure our hearts. It is a myth that human nature is inherently good and not intrinsically evil. The writer of Proverbs warns us that there is a way that seems right to a person, but the destination is death and destruction. As a result, the heart is an unreliable guidepost. We must allow God, not society or ourselves, to direct our path.

Seeds to Plant, Water, and Ruminate:
Just because it makes me feel good in the moment, or because my intentions seem good, does not make it any less sinful.

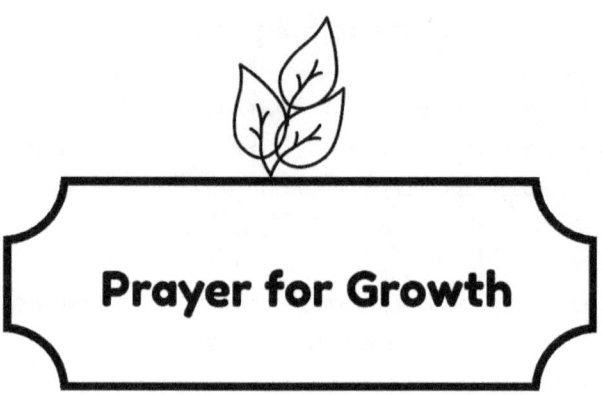

Prayer for Growth

Dear Wise and All-knowing God,

Thank You for the holy Scriptures. Your Word reveals Your love for me, the condition of my heart, and Your instructions on how to live. Lord, I want to seek You with my whole heart. Purify my heart from callousness, rebellion against Your Word, and selfishness. Please reveal the hidden motives in my heart that want to justify or rationalize different sins. Help me to understand and be grateful for the commands You have established; they are to benefit me, not to harm me.

In Jesus' name, amen.

Day 4: How Does Obedience Benefit Me?

Growth Scriptures:

"Those who love Your law have great peace, and nothing causes them to stumble."
-Psalm 119:165 NASB

"If Your law had not been my delight, Then I would have perished in my affliction."
-Psalm 119:92 NASB

Growth Insight: Obedience does not add or take anything away from God (Job 35:6-8). We are not doing God a favor by obeying His commands or following His will for our lives. Forgiving others gives us peace. It doesn't give God peace, nor does it rob God of peace. Keeping sexual intimacy within the confines of marriage protects us from disease and fosters emotional intimacy and security; it does protect God from disease or emotional damage. Choosing not to divorce gives our children and society stability; it doesn't stabilize God. When we lie, steal, cheat, mistreat others, refuse to repent, skip prayer, withhold love, or act selfishly, we hurt ourselves and others around us. God gives us instructions out of His love, passion, and compassion for us, not for His benefit. God's commands are there to free us, guide us, comfort us, motivate us, educate us, and to convict us, not to restrict us. Likewise, when God calls us to make some sort of leap of faith or life change, it always benefits us and those around us.

Seeds to Plant, Water, and Ruminate:
When I follow God's Word, I receive peace, healing, freedom, salvation, and joy.

Prayer for Growth

Dear Lord,

Thank You for Your many blessings and for Your guidance. Help me to see the Bible as a love story to me and all of Your children. Help me to rejoice in Your precepts and promises. Lord, I want to trust You and follow Your lead. Help me to see the endless blessings of Your Word and obedience to You. When I struggle to see the silver lining, remind me that You are for me. Give me the strength and courage to obey You when my faith is weak.

In Jesus' name, amen.

Day 5: Does the Clay Know More Than the Potter?

Growth Scriptures:

"But now, O Jehovah, thou art our Father; we are the clay, and thou our potter; and we all are the work of thy hand."
-Isaiah 64:8 ASB

"But who indeed are you, a human being, to talk back to God? Will what is made say to its maker, why have you created me so?"
-Romans 9:20 NAB

Growth Insight: Contrary to what society attempts to portray as fact, we are not here by an accidental, evolutionary, or spontaneous process. God crafted us and all the elements of the universe. We must not fail to remember that God is the potter, and we are the clay. It is He who made us for His purposes and by His design. God created us and knows our weaknesses, needs, strengths, and how we best function. We are not the author nor the final authority of our lives. No matter how wise and knowledgeable we think we have become, there is still information we are missing and things no one can comprehend except for God. God tells us His ways and thoughts are different and higher than ours (Isaiah 55:8-9). Additionally, we are advised to not think more highly of ourselves than we should (Romans 12:3). With our limited insight, it is sometimes difficult to not question God or have doubts. However, God is not out of touch with us or behind the times. He does not lack empathy. God created us with purpose and knows how the story ends. He knows us better than we know ourselves. He knows what's best for us and loves us.

Seeds to Plant, Water, and Ruminate:
Yes, God does understand my situation, and His commands still apply to me.

Prayer for Growth

Dear Creator of Heaven and Earth,

I am grateful that You have carefully crafted me and created me with a purpose. I am valuable because You have assigned me worth. You intervene on my behalf and are not aloof. Please forgive me when I second-guess Your Word, plan, abilities, motives, or love. Help me to operate in obedience to You. Mold me into what You want me to be because, I know it is more beautiful than anything I could construct or imagine.

In Jesus' name, amen.

Day 6: How Can God Really Relate to Me and Understand How Hard It Is?

Growth Scripture:

"For we do not have a high priest who is unable to empathize with our weaknesses, but we have one who has been tempted in every way, just as we are—yet he did not sin."
-Hebrews 4:15 NIV

Growth Insight: Growing up, we have all thought, at one time or another, that our parents (or guardians) couldn't possibly understand what we are going through. It is difficult to imagine that those in positions of authority ever experienced anything remotely similar to the struggles we have. We reason that if they did have similar hardships, then they would surely think and respond in the same manner as us. Right? Similarly, some people wonder how God can require so much of them when He never had to experience life as a human or fulfill the same requirements. However, this is not true. Jesus is a part of the Godhead Trinity. Scripture tells us that Jesus was tempted in every way but did not sin. In addition to not sinning, He also met all the requirements of the Old Testament Law.

Jesus came down to earth, was betrayed, spat on, flogged, mocked, lied on, rejected, beaten, stripped, nailed to a cross, and either bled to death, succumbed to organ failure, or suffocated on the cross. He experienced loss of loved ones and the physical limitations and ailments of life. Jesus is empathetic because he had a human body and lived among mankind. It is for this reason, that Jesus will be the judge on the throne on Judgement Day. The other members of the Trinity had to experience the separation from Jesus and allow Him to suffer punishment without intervention. Life was not easy for Jesus, which often caused Him to pray, recite Scripture, and fast for strength to make it through. The miracles He performed were to benefit others, not Himself.

Seeds to Plant, Water, and Ruminate:

Jesus can relate to my struggle with temptation and my physical and emotional suffering.

Dear Triune God,

Thank You for Your saving grace. I am thankful that You are a God who can empathize with my suffering and who loves me despite my disobedience. You have not asked me to meet expectations that You have not already fulfilled. Thank You for sending Jesus to deliver me from my sins. Christ suffered so that I could have eternal life, which is a debt I can never repay or truly comprehend. Please help me to honor this sacrifice by obeying Your Word. Help me to see and experience Your Word as truth.

In Jesus' name, amen.

Day 7: What If I Don't Obey?

Growth Scripture:

"They acted like fools in their rebellious ways, and suffered because of their sins."
-Psalm 107:17 NET

Growth Insight: Disobeying God may provide some temporary relief or pleasure, but it ultimately leads to a life of discontentment and dishonors God. When you do not obey God, you miss out on the many blessings He has in store for you such as knowing your purpose, understanding your worth, emotional healing, peace, wisdom, authentic love, true joy, healthy relationships, protection, provision, and intimacy with God. When you disobey God, you are out of His will for your life, and you do not feel His presence or guidance. Disobedience also leaves you open to emotional suffering and vulnerable to the lies and traps of the Enemy. Satan will have you believing that you are alone, that you are worthless, that you have no purpose, that you should live it up without fear of consequences, that your gender and sexual orientation are fluid, that drugs and alcohol will take away your pain, that marriage has no value and doesn't work, that fornication is fulfilling, that money and possessions are the most important things, and that how you treat others doesn't matter. Additionally, disobedience hinders your ability to introduce unbelievers to Christ and to reveal God's life transformation. Most importantly, when you disobey God, you miss opportunities to show that you love Him, that you are grateful to Him, that He is your Lord, and that You trust Him.

Seeds to Plant, Water, and Ruminate:
Disobedience to God will leave me confused, empty, broken, and disconnected from God.

Prayer for Growth

Dear God of Love and Mercy,

Please show grace to me when I am out of Your will for my life. Lead me back to Your path when I go astray. Help me to understand that chasing the things of this world will only lead to emptiness, disappointment, discontentment, brokenness, worthlessness, anxiety, depression, loneliness, and trouble. Only You can fulfill my deepest needs and desires. Only you can provide me with true joy, peace, worth, purpose, hope, love, protection, and salvation. Show me Your truth and bathe me in Your Word. Give me the desire to obey You in the face of temptation and the ability to discern negative societal influences. Thank You for Your patience with me, Your love for me, and Your kindnesses.

In Jesus' name, I pray. Amen.

Obey Challenge: Week 5

Discover How to Use Your Armor to Fight

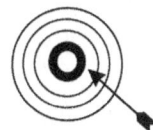

The rationale behind the challenge:

It is nearly impossible to resist and evade the pitfalls of sin when we do not possess the appropriate weapons or knowledge of how to utilize them properly. The aim of this challenge is to learn how to use the armor of God to fight sin and the schemes of the Enemy so that you can remain steadfast on the path of obedience. God did not leave you defenseless or alone in your battle against temptation, lies, confusion, hardship, adversity, and societal pressure. The belt of truth, breastplate of righteousness, sword of the spirit, shield of faith, gospel of peace, and helmet of salvation are powerful and effective in maintaining and strengthening your mental, emotional, and spiritual wellbeing. This week, you will examine the significance of each spiritual weapon and gain an understanding of how to apply them to situations you may encounter. As you begin to master the application of the armor of God, you will grow in your understanding of God and your Christian faith.

Growth Scripture:

"Henceforth be empowered in the Lord and in the strength of His might. Put on the complete armor of God, for you to be able to stand against the schemes of the devil."
-Ephesians 6:10-11 BLB

Day 1: How Do I Use the Belt of Truth and Sword of the Spirit?

Growth Scripture:

"Indeed, the word of God is living and active and sharper than any two-edged sword, piercing until it divides soul from spirit, joints from marrow; it is able to judge the thoughts and intentions of the heart."
-Hebrews 4:12 NRSV

Growth Insight: Never forget that Satan knows Scripture, maybe even better than you do, and is skilled at the art of manipulation. Jesus warns us that Satan is the author of lies. We have to study our Word in order to fight back. The sword of the Spirit is referred to as the Word of God (Ephesians 6:17). It is the only offensive weapon listed in the Armor of God passage. All the other weapons shield us from attacks. Satan twisted Scripture when he tempted Eve in the garden and Jesus in the wilderness. The Enemy knows that God's Word is a powerful weapon and tries to imitate it.

The belt of truth holds the sword of the Spirit and serves as its foundation. When we line ourselves with the truth revealed in the Scriptures, then Satan's weapons are deemed powerless. That's why the Enemy works so hard to have others discredit the Bible or to misuse it. If we can't recognize the truth, then we allow the lies to penetrate our hearts and minds.

The Word and truth work together. When we're not laced with the truth that God paid a hefty price for us, then we don't pick up the sword to cut down the lie that we're worthless. If we don't know God's promises, then we'll be left in confusion by believing and waiting for something God never said would happen. We are not defenseless or helpless. Remember God arms us with His Word and it's not dead. It's alive, active, and potent. Pick up your Sword and guard yourself with the truth.

Seeds to Plant, Water, and Ruminate:
Jesus is the Word and the Truth. My sword and my shield. My protection and weapon of choice.

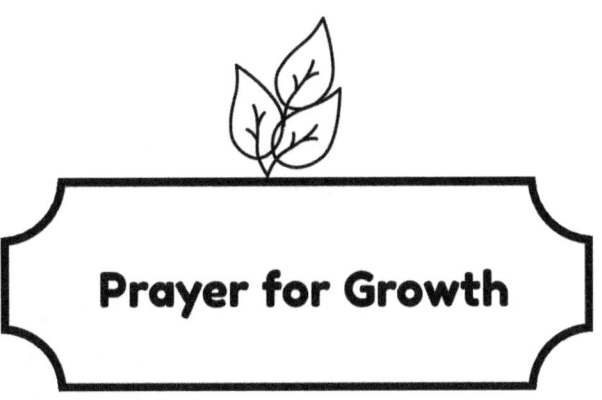

Prayer for Growth

Dear Lord,

The Almighty One, You are my refuge, strong tower, sword, and shield. Thank You for protecting me and not leaving me alone and defenseless. Please open my eyes to the truth of Your holy Scriptures and allow it to penetrate my heart. Help me to discern the lies, tricks, and traps that Satan and society present as truth. Expose the impure motives of others. When I am tested, help me to remember the truth concerning Your authority, promises, love, strength, and commands.

In Jesus' name, amen.

Day 2: How Do Use the Breastplate of Righteousness?

Growth Scripture:

"Stand firm then, with the belt of truth buckled around your waist, with the breastplate of righteousness arrayed."
-Ephesians 6:14 BSB

Growth Insight: The breastplate is armor that is designed to protect the body's major organs. This ancient equipment could withstand indirect hits from arrows and swords. That means that the tricks and the weapons you don't anticipate or see coming are deflected. In biblical times, the Romans used a breastplate with metal scaling, which could expose vulnerabilities and weaknesses. Hence, we have to be careful not to arm ourselves with our own righteousness so that attacks won't pierce through. Remember that our righteousness is like filthy rags in God's sight (Isaiah 64:6). God's breastplate of righteousness is flawless. Thus, cover yourself with this free gift.

Our metaphoric gut and heart are located and shielded behind the breastplate. God's moral laws are said to be written on our hearts. We innately and intuitively know what's right and wrong. The breastplate of righteousness keeps the corruption from outside influences from penetrating the heart, which is the center of our emotions. When we have this armor on, we act out what God considers to be right, not what our feelings tells us is right. God's breastplate of righteousness allows us to be imitators of Christ's morals and behaviors instead of society's moral standards and pressures.

Seed to Plant, Water, and Ruminate:
I must cover myself with His righteousness and not my own.

Prayer for Growth

Dear Lord,

You are a holy and righteous God. Thank You for seeing Jesus' righteousness in place of the stains from my sins. Lord, I desire to live according to Your Word and will. Show me the right path to take and help me to resist the things that attempt to mislead and lure me away from You. There are so many negative influences that are trying to mold my mind and life. Help me to hear Your voice. Give me the strength and courage to live out Your truth and not justify my actions through societal norms.

In Jesus' name, amen.

Day 3: How Do Use the Gospel of Peace and Helmet of Salvation?

Growth Scripture:

"For our struggle is not against flesh and blood, but against the rulers, against the authorities, against the powers of this world's darkness, and against the spiritual forces of evil in the heavenly realms."
-Ephesians 6:12 BSB

Growth Insight: Paul instructs us to have our feet ready and fitted with the gospel of peace (Ephesians 6:15). What does this mean? It means that we should always be ready and willing to share the loving grace of our Savior and His plan for our salvation. The good news is that all people can be saved because Jesus died for the recompense of our sins. We are to have our footing in the gospel of peace. If we do not have a firm foundation, then we fall and struggle to fight and defend ourselves. Without a biblical foundation, we will not even know who it is we are truly fighting. We are at war with Satan, those he influences, demons, and sin. The gospel informs us that when we accept Christ as our Lord and Savior we are at peace with God, we do not have to face His wrath, and will not experience eternal damnation.

We must also guard our heads with the helmet of salvation (Ephesians 6:17). The helmet protects our thoughts and beliefs. If we are not armed with the helmet of salvation, then we may be deceived into believing that we are fighting a losing battle and that we are in it alone. Jesus has already defeated sin, death, and the wicked spiritual forces of the world. However, at our vantage point, we haven't seen how everything plays out yet. Our salvation rests safely in His hands and cannot be snatched away (John 10:27-29). We have peace of mind knowing that Jesus died so that we can be forgiven of our sins and have eternal life with Him.

Seeds to Plant, Water, and Ruminate:
The conflict that I am experiencing is not really about the other person or situation. It's about discovering how Satan is trying to manipulate the circumstances and how the two of us can peacefully resolve the issue together.

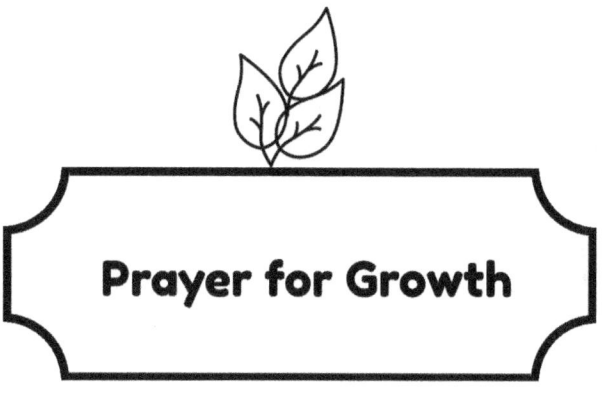

Dear Lord,

Thank You for Your saving grace and Jesus' sacrifice. Thank You for the peace of knowing that my salvation is secure in Your sovereign hands. Help me to not be inclined to war against my parent, spouse, child, employer, family, or friend. Lord, I want to aspire towards peace and to be in one accord with those in my life. Grant me with discernment to recognize when the Enemy is using lies to try to pit me against others or come to inaccurate conclusions. Strengthen me to come alongside others as we battle sinful influences, temptations, insecurities, inadequacies, and the issues of life.

I ask these things is Jesus' name, amen.

Day 4: How Do I Use the Shield of Faith?

Growth Scripture:

"In every situation take the shield of faith, and with it you will be able to extinguish all the flaming arrows of the evil one."
-Ephesians 6:16 HCSB

Growth Insight: The shield of faith is a versatile and powerful weapon. It can defend against both long-range and close-range attacks. That is to say, there are some things that are an immediate threat and others that are designed to damage us in the long run. Some threats are inconspicuous, and others are stealthily disguised. Paul tells us that the shield has the capability to extinguish all fiery arrows from the Enemy. That means the shield of faith can block the deadliest weapons and head-on attacks. Arrows can take the form of loss, trauma, mental and physical illness, experiencing hardships and injustices, others twisting Scripture, misinterpretation of our circumstances, and others trying to discredit our faith. Faith allows us to kill the lies, fears, confusion, and doubts. Whenever something approaches that is contrary to our faith, we have a firm enough foundation to wield our shield and stop it in its tracks.

Faith, at its core, is our belief that God is who He says He is, does what He says He will do, and has done what He says He has done. Faith assures us that the Scriptures are true and that our salvation is secure. When we are strong in faith, we believe that God is good, omnipotent, merciful, faithful, unfailing, reliable, in control, and will intervene on our behalf. Faith causes us to trust that God's commands are for our benefit and that He does not have ill-will towards us. When we have faith, we affirm God's deity, authority, dominion, justice, honesty, and perfection. We trust that God is wise, eternal, and intentional. He provides us with provision, protection, pathways, promises, prosperity, and purpose. We believe that He created the entire universe and that there is no God but Him. Faith persuades us to not waver in our trust that God created us with intrinsic worth and blesses us with His self-sacrificial love.

Seeds to Plant, Water, and Ruminate:
The same God that is omnipresent, omnipotent, and omniscient shields me, sees me, knows me, saves me, loves me, and aids me.

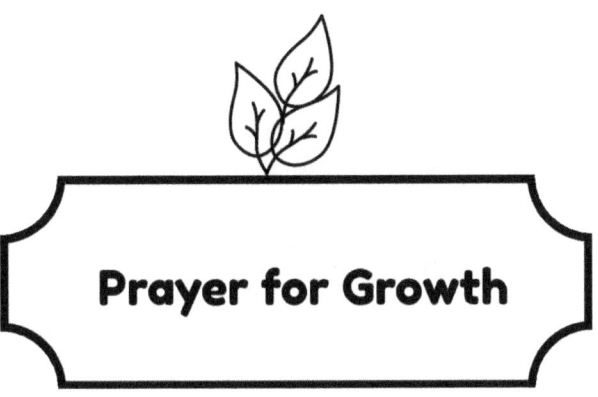

Prayer for Growth

Dear Lord,

I am so grateful that You are an omnipotent God, yet loving and self-sacrificial. Thank You for being a God of truth and a God who keeps His promises. Strengthen my faith, Lord, so that I am not deceived or discouraged by others. Help me to interpret situations through Your eyes and Your Word. Show me the truth when others attempt to discredit You or falsely present the Scriptures. Lord, help me to believe that You are working on something beautiful for me when I can only see the disarray. Remind me that You are my everything and all that I need.

In Jesus' name, amen.

Day 5: How Do I Use Prayer as a Weapon?

Growth Scriptures and Growth Quote:

"Confess your sins to one another and pray for one another, that you may be healed. The insistent prayer of a righteous person is powerfully effective."
-James 5:16 WEB

"The weapons of our warfare are not the weapons of the world. Instead, they have divine power to demolish strongholds. We tear down arguments and every presumption set up against the knowledge of God; and we take captive every thought to make it obedient to Christ."
-2 Corinthians 10:4-5 BSB

"If you are a stranger to prayer, you are a stranger to the greatest source of power known to human beings."
-Billy Sunday

Growth Insight: Prayer is the ultimate weapon in our fight against the Enemy. It's like using the trump card, bringing out the unbeatable final boss in a video game, or calling in the tanks and air support. Imagine the scenes in the movie where it appears that battle and all hope is lost. Then the cavalry comes riding in, over the hills, to save the day. When we can no longer put up a fight, and there is no one else to offer assistance, God can fight on our behalf. Prayer is often used as the last line of defense but is available to us throughout the battle and before it even begins. Prayer is also like firing a flare gun or sending out a war cry to God. Subsequently, it's game over when He intervenes.

Prayer is not listed as a part of the armor of God, but Paul mentions it in the same passage. He instructs us to pray in the spirit during all circumstances. James also informs believers that prayers from righteous people are powerful and prevail. Remember, we are not righteous in and of ourselves, but we wear God's breastplate of righteous. Therefore, our prayers can accomplish much. Prayer can cover our exposed areas and blind spots and patch up our wounds and the weaknesses in the armor.

Seeds to Plant, Water, and Ruminate:
My prayers have power to change the situation and to change me in the situation.

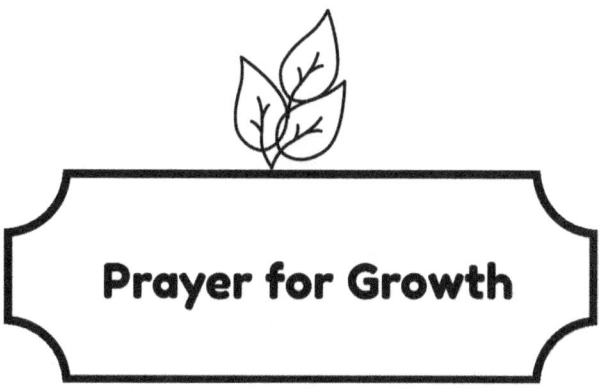

Dear Lord,

You are a living God who is active in my life. You have granted me access to You through the Holy Spirit and prayer. Please protect my mind and my heart as the Enemy tries to make me doubt Your goodness, love, promises, strength, Word, truth, and will. Help me to feel Your presence and to comprehend how You have answered my prayers. I trust in Your wisdom, compassion, and power.

I ask these things in Jesus' mighty name, amen.

Day 6: Don't Fight Alone

Growth Scriptures:

"A person standing alone can be attacked and defeated, but two can stand back-to-back and conquer. Three are even better, for a triple-braided cord is not easily broken."
-Ecclesiastes 4:12 NLT

"'They will fight against you but will never overcome you, since I am with you to deliver you,' declares the LORD."
-Jeremiah 1:19 BSB

Growth Insight: You need someone to have your back; it's exposed. During the Roman Empire, the soldiers would fight back-to-back to protect the region of the body without armor. This formation also allowed fellow soldiers to help defend one another from attacks that they could not see nor anticipate. Two sets of eyes are better than one. As believers in Christ, we have to look out for one another. When we see that our brothers and sisters, in Christ, are misusing armor, missing armor, have damaged armor, or using the incorrect armor, then we should aid them. We should not ridicule, abandon, or wage against them. Cover them with your shield and prayers. Teach and encourage them with love. Model proper use with transparency and humility. Sometimes we have to carry some spare equipment and help others get dressed.

Other times, we're the ones that need help. Battle can become exhausting. There are times when we need someone else to help hold us up and empower us to keep going. It's important to hold each other accountable for actions and spiritual growth. Let's support one another and invite God's presence into the battle. With God, we are never truly alone.

Seeds to Plant, Water, and Ruminate:
Help others because God helps us. When we help others to grow, we grow ourselves.

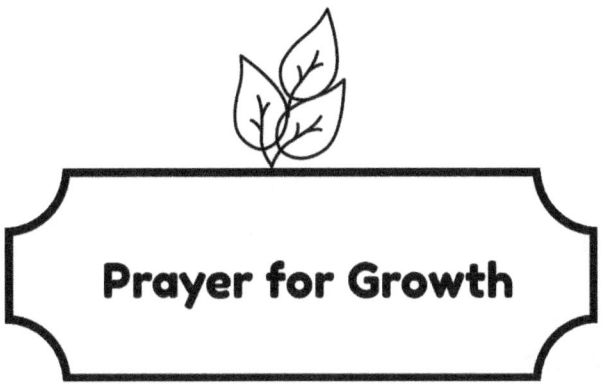

Prayer for Growth

Dear God,

You are a loving father and a friend. You are a comforter and a guide. You fight for me and beside me. Thank You for not leaving me to fight and carry burdens on my own. Enable me to accept and ask for help when I need it. Endow me with the strength, patience, grace, courage, and wisdom I need to aid others in their journey with You and with life circumstances.

In Jesus' name, I pray. Amen.

Day 7: Fully Suit Up Daily

Growth Scripture:

"Therefore take up the full armor of God, so that when the day of evil comes, you will be able to stand your ground, and having done everything, to stand."
-Ephesians 6:13 MSB

Growth Insight: When we put on the full armor of God, then we are completely equipped to fight and stand our ground against the Evil One. We cannot be halfway armed when our adversary attacks us. The helmet of salvation, breastplate of righteousness, shield of faith, belt of truth, sword of the spirit, and the gospel of peace are all interconnected, interdependent, and work together. We need each weapon at all times. Missing just one of these components will leave you vulnerable in a battle. Without the helmet of salvation or the shield of faith, we don't even know that we have the ability to win the fight or where our power and strength come from. Without the belt of truth or sword of the spirit, we can't distinguish the truth from the lies. Lastly, without the gospel of peace or the breastplate of righteousness, we are unaware of what and whom we're truly fighting and unsure of the proper moral conduct we should display.

We have to stay armed and on guard because we never know the trick, person, lie, trap, tragedy, circumstance, or place Satan will employ to harm us. Pop culture can misguide and mold our beliefs through use of social media, popular tv shows, movies, book series, music, and advertisements. Guard your ears, eyes, mind, and hearts so that you do not allow lies and temptation to creep in. Even when we are around our friends, co-workers, family, or significant others, we still cannot remove our armor. Satan knows that these people impact us the most and can intentionally or unintentionally hurt us deeply. Consequently, we have to evaluate each of our interactions using God's truth and righteousness. Otherwise, we'll feel defeated, think we are hopeless and helpless, be led astray, believe right is wrong, or put on the chains of sin.

Seeds to Plant, Water, and Ruminate:

I must be on guard at all times because sin tries to disguise itself as harmless and takes on many unsuspecting forms.

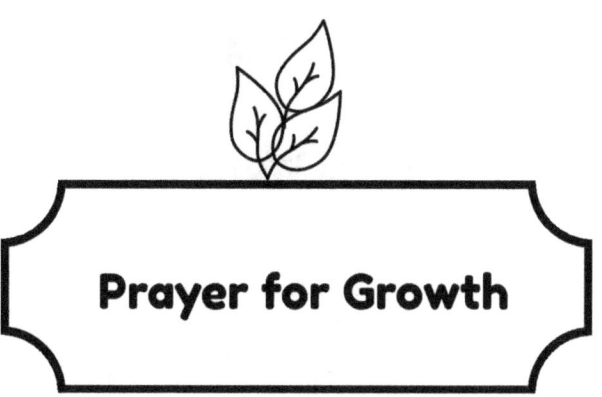

Prayer for Growth

Dear Lord,

You are my Shepherd. Your sheep hear and know Your voice. Help me to block out any voice or influence that is not in line with You. Allow Your Word and authority to reign supreme over my life. Reveal any sin that I have in my heart and give me the will, strength, and wisdom to fight against it. Help me to decipher the sin, threats, and traps. Forgive me of any sin that I let fester and aid me in turning away from it.

In Jesus' name, amen.

Step 4: Worship

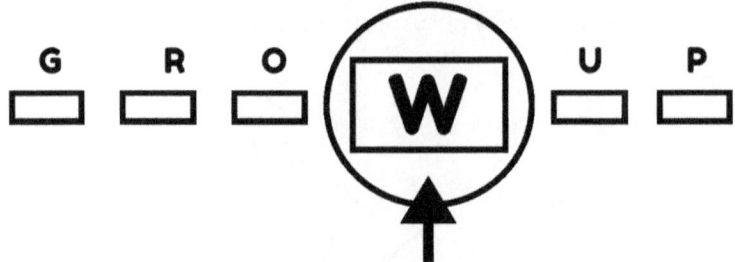

What Is Worship?

Worship is an inward and outward response of honor and reverence to God. It esteems His essence, supreme authority, and deity. God's presence should evoke a physical, mental, and emotional reaction within us. In biblical passages such as Psalm 95, worship was synonymous with bowing down, kneeling and/or lying prostrate before God. Traditionally, the English meaning of worship has been offering homage to a worthy God. Modern worship has now morphed worship into the inclusion of practices such as prayer, giving, singing, lifting of hands, playing instruments, Scripture reading, and committing oneself to a lifestyle of obedience to God. During worship, we lower ourselves and exalt God as holy and superior. True worship surrenders the heart, mind, spirit, desire, and will to God.

Growth Scripture:

"I am the Lord your God, who brought you out of the land of Egypt, out of the house of bondage. You shall have no other gods before Me. You shall not make for yourself a carved image—any likeness of anything that is in heaven above, or that is in the earth beneath, or that is in the water under the earth; you shall not bow down to them nor serve them. For I, the Lord your God, am a jealous God, visiting the iniquity of the fathers upon the children to the third and fourth generations of those who hate Me, but showing mercy to thousands, to those who love Me and keep My commandments."
-Exodus 20:2-6 NKJV

Worship Challenge: Week 6

Discover Your *Why* and *How* to Worship

The rationale behind the challenge:

The objective of this challenge is to paint a clear picture of godly worship, convey the cruciality of worship, and to ignite a strong propensity to worship. One of the many reasons we were created is to worship our Creator. Once you come to the realization of how much God is deserving of your worship, your eyes will be opened to the immensity of the grace, mercy, and blessings He affords you. Gratitude for a worthy God and a sense of purpose are great propellants of spiritual growth and intimacy with God.

Growth Quote:

"Here is my Creed. I believe in one God, the Creator of the Universe. That He governs it by His Providence. That He ought to be worshipped. That the most acceptable service we render to him is in doing good to his other children."
-Benjamin Franklin

Day 1: Read and Study the Bible

Growth Scripture and Growth Quotes:

"This Book of the Law must not depart from your mouth; meditate on it day and night, so that you may be careful to do everything written in it. For then you will prosper and succeed in all you do."
-Joshua 1:8 MSB

"Reading Christians are growing Christians. When Christians cease to read, they cease to grow."
-John Wesley

"Study to know Him more and more, for the more you know, the more you will love Him."
-George Whitefiled

Growth Insight: In our culture, one way to honor individuals is to grant them with respect of our listening ear. In the book of Joshua, Joshua bows down with his face to the ground and asks God, "What has my Lord to say to his servant?" (Joshua 5:14). Honoring God is to not only hear what He says but to adhere to what He says. The Bible is God's Word and it should speak to us and move us to action. Don't just skim or read the Bible—study it, memorize it, and meditate on it.

Reading the Bible is not merely a fifteen-minute exercise to check off your to-do list and move on with your day. The message of the Bible is something that should guide, motivate, convict, and encourage us throughout the day. Thus, have a heart of delight as you read. View the Bible as something vitality important and beneficial, not a chore or burden. Remember the Bible is for you. It doesn't affect God if you don't read it; it hurts you. Not studying the Bible deprives you of understanding God's love for you, discovering His salvation plan for you, learning from the mistakes of other believers, knowing God's expectations on how you are to live your life, and comprehending your purpose and worth.

Seeds to Plant, Water, and Ruminate:
I honor God by studying, obeying, and treasuring his Word in my heart.

Prayer for Growth

Dear Lord,

I honor and respect You. I am thankful for the privilege of reading the Scriptures, which are Your love letters to me. Your Word is important and authoritative in my life. It gives me insight on how to live a life pleasing to You. As I study, I pray that Your Word changes my heart, helps my relationship with You to grow, opens my eyes to Your goodness and grace, and increases my trust in Your power and plan for me. I want to yearn for You and love Your Word. Help me to be receptive of what You have to say.

In Jesus' name, I pray. Amen.

Day 2: Sing, Dance, Bow, Shout, and Lift Your Hands

Growth Scriptures:

"Oh come, let's sing to Yahweh. Let's shout aloud to the rock of our salvation! Oh come, let's worship and bow down. Let's kneel before Yahweh, our Maker."
-Psalm 95:1,6 WEB

"And David danced before Jehovah with all his might; and David was girded with a linen ephod. So David and all the house of Israel brought up the ark of Jehovah with shouting, and with the sound of the trumpet."
-2 Samuel 6:14-15 ASV

Growth Insight: Another way to worship God is through music and dance. The book of Psalms is filled with beautiful illustrations of godly praise and worship. It gives instructions for people to sing, dance, shout, lift their hands, play instruments, and bow down to God. We use songs to declare God as Lord and Savior, to express our adoration, convey gratitude, acknowledge His great works, and to reiterate our acceptance of His call. There are also examples of biblical figures lying prostrate with their faces to the ground, which is a position of worship and submission. Lifting our hands and bowing is a sign of honor and surrender to His presence, influence, and authority. Shouting, playing instruments, and singing celebrates and proclaims who God is, what He has done, and what He will do.

Seeds to Plant, Water, and Ruminate:
God is deserving of all of our worship, yet He is not in need of it. God is so good that as we worship God, we are blessed.

Prayer for Growth

Dear Lord of Heaven and Earth,

Creator of the Universe, and Lord of Angel Armies, You are worthy of the highest praise. Thank You for the joy, inspiration, comfort, and closeness that comes from worshipping You through music, vocalizations, and positions of reverence. I pray that You are pleased with my offering of worship. Let me not neglect to give you the respect You deserve, nor fail to remember the magnitude of eminence, holiness, and majesty.

In Jesus' name, amen.

Day 3: Worship Through Art, Prayer, and Writing

Growth Scriptures:

"When I behold Your heavens, the work of Your fingers, the moon and the stars, which You have set in place—what is man that You are mindful of him, or the son of man that You care for him?"
-Psalm 8:3-4 MSB

"The heavens declare the glory of God; the skies proclaim the work of His hands. Day after day they pour forth speech; night after night they reveal knowledge. Without speech or language, without a sound to be heard their voice has gone out into all the earth, their words to the ends of the world."
-Psalm 29:1-4 BSB

Growth Insight: Writing prayers, songs, and poems about God, and to Him, is also a form of worship. The book of Psalms is filled with heartfelt poems and songs that were designed to be sung and performed with music. The writers honor God by using titles of reverence and majesty. They glorify God by thanking Him and telling of His greatness and good works. In these writings, the psalmists lower themselves and elevate God's position and supremacy. Through writing prayers, we are better able to reflect on the condition of our hearts and our attitude towards God. When we write our prayers, we converse with God and communicate our devotion to Him, our respect for His Lordship, and our submission to His authority. Worship focuses on giving God the homage that He is due, which can be achieved through writing and art.

God Himself is an artist, and we are made in His image. He magnificently designed and sculpted creation with meticulous detail. Taking care of the earth and beautifying it demonstrates that we are appreciative of the world God created for us. Designing and erecting a place of worship can also be done to honor God. Creating drawings and paintings that depict biblical principles can bring glory to God. These works of art can express our love for God and inspire others to be in awe of God. Developing coloring pages for little ones to help them learn about God and express themselves can also be considered an act of worship. Artistic expression is a form of worship that deepens our connection to our Creator.

Seeds to Plant, Water, and Ruminate:
God is so great and creative that He made us with the ability to create and interpret symbols and letters into art and language. Use these gifts to worship the Creator, not the created things.

Dear Lord,

The greatness of Your beauty, knowledge, and power cannot be comprehended. Thank You for the variety within Your magnificent creation. Enable me to use any writing skills or artistic abilities to honor You and to spread Your love and Gospel to others. Let my heart be overwhelmed with gratitude on even the darkest of days. You are my light, my rock, and my salvation.

I ask these things in Jesus' name, amen.

Day 4: Worship Through a Lifestyle of Obedience

Growth Scripture:

"Therefore I urge you, brothers, on account of God's mercy, to offer your bodies as living sacrifices, holy and pleasing to God, which is your spiritual service of worship."
-Romans 12:1 BSB

Growth Insight: Worship is a lifestyle and state of mind. We are to present ourselves before our King in daily worship. Each day, where we go, what we do, what we listen to, what we watch, what we say, how we process our circumstances, and how we perceive the world around us matters. These things should be a reflection of our surrendered heart, allegiance to God, obedience to His Word and will, and reverence for who He is. We are to live our lives in such a way that it brings honor and glory to His name. Loving God, serving His people, and giving up our sins is done out of respect for who God is. We sacrifice our will and desires because we exalt Him as higher than ourselves. In addition to flesh and bones, our bodies encompass mind and spirit. Therefore, we must set apart our physical bodies, actions, and thoughts for God's purposes, honor, and praise. We are not our own. We are His servants and friends.

Seeds to Plant, Water, and Ruminate:
I worship my Master by obeying Him, displaying love to others, and living a life of holiness and integrity.

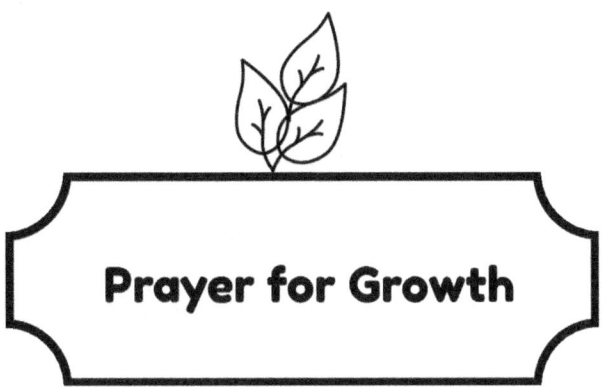

Prayer for Growth

Dear Sovereign God,

You have no equal. Your Word is true and good. Help me to honor You with my life. Let my life be a song of praise and worship to You. Remind me that You are the Lawgiver and Potter; I am the servant and clay. Continue to mold me to look more Christ-like. Help me to bend my will and desires to Yours. Help me to hate sin and to love You.

In Jesus' name, amen.

Day 5: Worship Through Giving

Growth Scriptures:

"Let each man give according as he has determined in his heart, not grudgingly or under compulsion, for God loves a cheerful giver."
-2 Corinthians 9:7 WEB

"Honor the LORD with your wealth and with the firstfruits of all your harvest."
-Proverbs 3:9 MSB

"And do not neglect to do good and to share with others, for with such sacrifices God is pleased."
-Hebrews 13:16 MSB

Growth Insight: Giving is a way to worship our Creator and Savior. When Jesus was born, the wise men from the East brought gifts to honor Him as King. Out of respect for the Provider and Lawgiver, the Israelites brought sacrifices and burnt offerings to the temple's altar. In the Old Testament, believers tithed a tenth of their crops and livestock in order that the temple priests and Levites would be taken care of. What God asks of us is never for His sake; it is used to bless ourselves and others. In Matthew 25, Jesus states that if we give to the needy, then it is as though we are giving to Him. Giving our time, talents, and treasures to our local church to support ministries and programs is also a way to show reverence to God. In Scripture, there are examples of people coming before kings with gifts. How much more deserving of gifts is our King of Kings? Give from your heart, not begrudgingly, out of obligation, or fear of retribution. God loves a cheerful giver.

Seeds to Plant, Water, and Ruminate:
I can never repay God for His sacrifice for me or for the countless blessings He's given me. Out of gratitude and respect, I should give Him my best gifts.

Prayer for Growth

Dear King of Kings and Lord of Lords,

Thank You for Your great gifts. Thank You for the opportunity to be a blessing to others. I want to honor You through giving You my time, talent, and treasure. Everything I have is because of You and belongs to You. Help me to not hoard what you have entrusted me with. Strengthen my trust that You will continue to take care of my needs.

In Jesus' name, amen.

Day 6: Heart of Worship

Growth Scripture:

"These people honor Me with their lips, but their hearts are far from Me. They worship Me in vain; they teach as doctrine the precepts of men."
-Matthew 15:8-9 BSB

Growth Insight: Worship is more about the heart of the worshipper than about the act itself. God doesn't want us to bow, kneel, pray, give, praise, dance, or sing out of mere ritual; He wants our hearts. God desires a humbled and surrendered heart. As we worship, we acknowledge His superiority, authority, power, and divinity. We honor Him with a heart of humility, gratitude, awe, and servitude. Jesus said that we must worship Him in spirit and truth. Worship should be authentic and out of love, admiration, devotion, and respect for God. That is to say, that we are to have true faith in the Triune God and His holy Word. It requires that we come to God with honesty and a sincere desire to glorify, obey, and know Him. Seek His truth, not what we hope to be true, in order to justify ourselves.

Throughout worship, we allow the Holy Spirit to increase, work within us, convict our hearts, and cause us to take action. God does not want your gift, or other forms of worship, if your motives are impure or if you have unrepentant sin in your heart. During the Sermon on the Mount, Jesus advises us to resolve our conflicts with one another before we even present our offerings to God (Matthew 5:23-24). As you worship, search your heart and reflect on your adherence to His Word and attitude towards Him.

Seeds to Plant, Water, and Ruminate:
God wants my heart!

Prayer for Growth

Dear God of Love,

I'm grateful that You desire an intimate relationship with me and not merely homage and obedience. I'm thankful that You are not aloof. You are my present help and You seek an authentic connection with me. Help me to yearn for You and to honor You with my gifts, servitude, love towards others, and adherence to Your Word. Purify my heart and cleanse me with Your truth so that I am pleasing to You.

In Jesus' name, amen.

Day 7: Don't Forsake the Gathering

Growth Scripture:

"Let's consider how to provoke one another to love and good works, not forsaking our own assembling together, as the custom of some is, but exhorting one another, and so much the more as you see the Day approaching."
-Hebrews 10:24-25 WEB

Growth Insight: There are many benefits of meeting together to worship God. God desires unity among His people. What a beautiful sight to see and hear God's children worshiping Him, as sovereign Lord, together. The followers of Christ are to be one church body that considers themselves close as brothers and sisters. God's spirit is within each of us. Therefore, when we worship together His presence is magnified.

Attending a church service combines multiple elements of worship: giving, praying, Scripture reading, singing, playing music, bowing, lifting hands, and more. These activities bring honor to God, but they also build up the body of believers. Worship services provide an opportunity to serve one another with our spiritual gifts. Through use of our gifts, we encourage, support, and teach one another. Joining a body of believers assists with the sharing of knowledge and resources that aids in furthering God's kingdom. Fellowship and worship help us to become closer to God and grow deeper in our faith.

Seeds to Plant, Water, and Ruminate:
As I pour into others, God pours into me. I grow as I help others to grow.

Prayer for Growth

Dear Lord,

I thank You for the believers that You have placed in my life to foster my growth in You. I pray that I do not take the support of others for granted or keep the gifts and blessings You granted me to myself. Give me the strength, patience, and wisdom that I need to serve and work with those advancing Your kingdom. Help me to see the benefits and to take delight in worshipping with my brothers and sisters in Christ.

In Jesus' name, amen.

Step 5: Use Spiritual Gifts

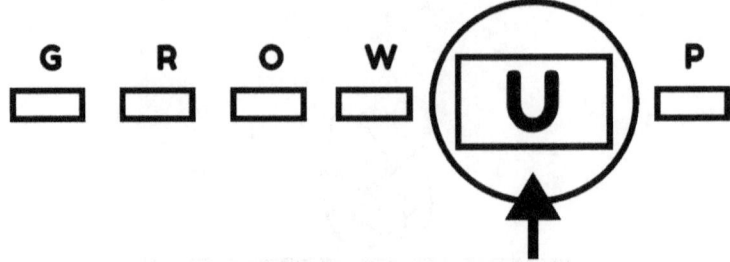

What Does It Mean To Use My Spiritual Gifts?

Another huge step on your journey to spiritual growth involves the actualization and the utilization of your gifts, talents, strengths, and skills for God's glory. It is God who granted each of us with these attributes and predestined us to use them. We are charged with the responsibility and privilege to dedicate these blessings to a life of service to our Master and Maker.

Growth Quote:

"Lord, I am no longer my own, but Yours. Put me to what You will, rank me with whom You will. Let be employed by You or laid aside for You, exalted for You or brought low by You. Let me have all things, let me have nothing, I freely and heartily yield all things to Your pleasure and disposal. And now, O glorious and blessed God, Father, Son, and Holy Spirit, You are mine and I am Yours. So be it. Amen."
-John Wesley

Growth Scripture:

"I planted the seed and Apollos watered it, but God made it grow. So neither he who plants nor he who waters is anything, but only God, who makes things grow."
-1 Corinthians 3:6-7 MSB

Use Your Spiritual Gifts Challenge: Week 7

Discover Your Purpose and Spiritual Gifts

The rationale behind the challenge:

In one form or another, every person has pondered the age-old conundrum: "What is my purpose and how do I fulfill it?" It seems to be the most puzzling and challenging concept that humans grapple with. This week you will explore why God created you, what He wants you to do while you are on earth, and how he has equipped you to do it. Understanding our purpose and our spiritual gifts gives us direction, motivation, and satisfaction. Using our gifts to serve God strengthens and grows our faith, character, focus on God, relationship with God, passion, love, gratitude, and our inner joy.

Growth Scripture:

"Before I formed you in the womb I knew you, and before you were born I set you apart and appointed you as a prophet to the nations."
-Jeremiah 1:5 MSB

Day 1: What Are Spiritual Gifts, and Do I Have One?

Growth Scripture:

"As each has received a gift, employ it in serving one another, as good managers of the grace of God in its various forms."
-1 Peter 4:10 WEB

Growth Insight: Spiritual gifts are abilities that God has given to His believers. These gifts are not earned through good merits, and you do not have to be a super-Christian to receive them. Scripture makes it clear that God has used His own wisdom and grace to grant every believer with at least one gift. No gift is better than the other and each gift serves its own important purpose in God's kingdom. Despite other people's opinions of you, or your own feelings of unworthiness and inadequacy, you have a spiritual gift and a unique role to play in using your gift to glorify God.

It is undetermined whether or not the lists of spiritual gifts, provided to us in the Bible, are exhaustive. Nonetheless, the specified spiritual gifts are as follows: mercy, prophecy, teaching, knowledge, faith, wisdom, discernment of spirits, leadership, exhortation, speaking in tongues, interpretation of tongues, apostleship, shepherding, giving, helping/serving, administration, evangelism, healing, and performing miracles (1 Corinthians 12, 1 Peter 4, Romans 12, Ephesians 4). The Holy Spirit empowers each member of the body of Christ to perform different functions to edify the church, serve God, and advance His message.

Seeds to Plant, Water, and Ruminate:
God has entrusted me with a gift to bring glory to His name, not my own.

Prayer for Growth

Dear Lord,

I thank You for not being a respecter of persons and that You give freely to all. Guard my heart so that I do not misuse the gifts You have bestowed upon me. I pray that I bring honor to You and edify the body of Christ as I serve them with my gifts. Remind me to praise and worship You with my gifts and to not worship the gifts themselves. Grant me with courage to use my gifts and wisdom to know when and how to use them.

In Jesus' name, amen.

Day 2: What's the Purpose of Spiritual Gifts?

Growth Scriptures:

"To equip the saints for works of ministry and to build up the body of Christ."
-Ephesians 4:12 MSB

"The Spirit's presence is shown in some way in each person for the good of all."
-1 Corinthians 12:7 GNT

Growth Insight: Spiritual gifts are designed to build up the body of believers, spread the gospel, and serve God. We are given gifts to help others, not to benefit ourselves. The Corinthian church had issues with individuals using their gifts to bring attention to themselves and to garner praise from others. Paul reminded these early church believers that spiritual gifts are to be used to edify one another and to help each other grow in faith. We are to remain humble because we did not acquire our gifts on our own; they were granted to us by God. Spiritual gifts should point believers and non-believers toward God's truth, goodness, grace, love, commands, and salvation. Although our gifts are for others, when we use our gifts to honor God, it somehow blesses us as well. We strengthen our own faith, increase our understanding, and become closer to God. When we use our gifts, it creates a sense of gratitude and satisfaction because we realize that we are carrying out our God-given purpose.

Seeds to Plant, Water, and Ruminate:
Although my spiritual gifts are a blessing to me and helps me to grow, they are intended for me to serve others and to help them grow.

Prayer for Growth

Dear Lord,

Thank You for Your attentiveness towards me and Your active presence in my life. When I can't see the big picture, help me to see You in the details. Through my gifts, empower me to lead others to Your truth, Your goodness, and a closer relationship with You. I pray that others experience Your love and see You working through me as I use my gifts. Forgive me for any impure motives, doubts, or haughtiness that emerges in my heart.

In Jesus' name, amen.

Day 3: Strengths, Talents, and Skills

Growth Scriptures:

"There are different gifts, but the same Spirit. There are different ministries, but the same Lord. There are different ways of working, but the same God works all things in all people."
-1 Corinthians 12:4-6 BSB

"Whatever you do, work at it with all your heart, as though you were working for the Lord and not for people."
-Colossians 3:23 GNT

Growth Insight: God made every person uniquely and purposefully. No two people have the same combination of strengths, talents, and skills. A skill is simply your ability to complete a task. It is something that you had to be taught to do. Strengths are character traits, thought patterns, or actions that are almost flawlessly applied on a consistent basis. These set of abilities are typically used to enhance our interactions with others or to benefit others in some capacity. Strengths can be improved with time and effort. Talents are abilities that are innately present; you were born with them. Usually, talents require some fine tuning and need to be honed in. Talents become strengths when they can be regularly, and appropriately, applied to situations at a high proficiency level. The work we do for God isn't only limited to using our spiritual gifts. There are many roles to fill and countless circumstances where our skills, talents, and strengths are needed. All of these abilities work together to help advance God's kingdom. Do all things in honor of our Lord, regardless of their perceived significance.

Seeds to Plant, Water, and Ruminate:
God can use me in the seemingly small, mundane, and unnoticed things. I can make a significant difference without doing something large scale or conspicuous.

Prayer for Growth

Dear Lord,

I thank You for being patient with me and providing me with Your grace. You are in the whisper as well as the storm. You are in the blade of grass as well as the mountain. Lord, help me to not deem certain tasks as too small or too great for Your kingdom and glory. Allow me to use my strengths, talents, and skills in a manner that is pleasing to You. Help me to serve with an attitude of gratitude, humility, and kindness. Remind me that I serve others out of respect for You, not because others are deserving or out of my own selfish desires.

In Jesus' mighty name, I pray. Amen.

Day 4: How Do I Use my Gifts, Talents, Strengths, and Skills?

Growth Scripture:

"For the body does not consist of one part, but of many. If the foot should say, 'Because I am not a hand, I do not belong to the body,' that would not make it any less a part of the body. And if the ear should say, 'Because I am not an eye, I do not belong to the body,' that would not make it any less a part of the body. If the whole body were an eye, where would the sense of hearing be? If the whole body were an ear, where would the sense of smell be?"
-1 Corinthians 12:14-17 BSB

Growth Insight: It is often said that the harvest is plentiful, but the laborers are few (Matthew 9:37). There is always work to do in God's kingdom, but not enough willing workers. Anything you do can be done for God's glory. Nothing is insignificant when you're doing it out of love and service to your Master. You can start by reaching out to your local church and inquiring about their volunteer needs. Maybe they need individuals to help clean, serve food, pass out materials, direct people to the right location, read announcements and Scriptures, or type up a bulletin. It doesn't require much skill to complete any of these tasks, but these things are needed and make an impact.

Strengths such as making others feel welcomed, being inclusive, having a high-spirited nature, and resolving conflicts can help to create an inviting environment, energize people for worship, mediate, encourage members to get involved, and empower others to do God's work and will. A person talented in writing could write church plays, newsletters, poems, songs, and Christian literature. Additionally, if you are talented with making crafts, entertaining children, playing an instrument, singing, dancing, managing money, creating art, then maybe participating in choir, bookkeeping, preparing children's activities, painting a mural, or praise dancing could be right for you.

If you have the gifts of speaking, teaching, knowledge, wisdom, encouragement, mercy, or evangelism, then preaching, teaching Sunday school, leading Bible study, mentoring, advising, or being a listening ear could be a good fit for you. Gifts of prayer, giving, serving, administration, and pastoring could be indicative of being capable of taking on roles as a prayer intercessor, benefactor, helper, clergy, coordinator, or administrator. Lastly, gifts of speaking in tongues (ability to speak a language that you did not learn), interpretation of tongues, healing, and performing miracles are useful during mission trips and community outreach.

Seeds to Plant, Water, and Ruminate:
With a heart of humility, love, integrity, and obedience, I can use any ability to bring God glory.

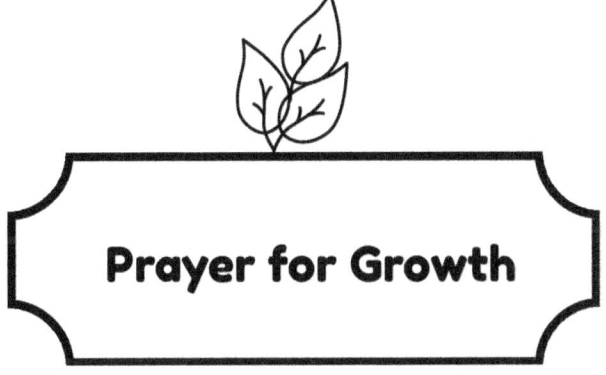

Prayer for Growth

Dear Lord,

My Rabboni, teach me Your ways and Your will for my life. Help me to follow Your lead as I serve and lead Your people. Show me how to incorporate the strengths, talents, gifts, and skills you have afforded me into Your kingdom. I offer You a heart of humility, surrender, and obedience. Use me for Your glory and purpose as You see fit. I desire to serve You with gratitude and gladness. Thank You for choosing me and saving me.

In Jesus' name, I pray. Amen.

Day 5: How Do I Discover My Unique Gifts, Talents and Strengths?

Growth Scriptures:

"I will instruct you and teach you in the way you should go; I will counsel you with my eye upon you."
-Psalm 32:8 ESV

"Lord, you have searched me and known me. For it was you who created my inward parts; you knit me together in my mother's womb. Your eyes saw me when I was formless; all my days were written in your book and planned before a single one of them began."
-Psalm 139:1,13,16 CSB

Growth Insight: Often, we struggle to recognize our own gifts, talents, and strengths. However, when other people ask us to tell them what we have observed their abilities to be, we can tell them with ease. In order to gain clarity on these issues, we can start by first asking our Creator. He designed you and knows you better than you know yourself. Pray and ask God to make it plain and clear to you. Next, you can ask for feedback from other believers. People who have seen us serving God can offer insight into the things we do well and how they have seen God use us to positively impact others. Additionally, you can analyze your passions and things that energize your spirit. When God places a godly mission or desire in our hearts, He grants us with the means to carry it out. Lastly, you can take a spiritual gift and strength assessment. Assessments help us to see attributes and their applications that we may have otherwise overlooked or minimized.

Seeds to Plant, Water, and Ruminate:
When I earnestly seek God's will, He will reveal to me how He intends to use me.

Prayer for Growth

Dear Heavenly Father,

Thank You for the opportunity to grow closer to You and mature in my Christian journey. You have granted me with capabilities that are unique to me. Open my eyes to perceive them and my heart to receive them. I pray that I remain humble so that I will not have to be humbled or cause others to turn away from the church. Help me to better understand the use and purpose of my gifts, strengths, and talents.

In Jesus' name, amen.

Day 6: What Is My Purpose?

Growth Scripture & Growth Quote:

"For we are His workmanship, having been created in Christ Jesus for good works which God prepared beforehand that we should walk in them."
-Ephesians 2:10 BLB

"The two most important days in your life are the day you are born and the day you find out why."
-Mark Twain

Growth Insight: The good news is that you have a purpose. You are significant, you matter, and you are valuable. We were all created for the same purpose. The goal is the same, but our objectives and assignments look slightly different from one another. God gave you a unique set of missions to bring Him glory. There is not merely just one thing that your whole life leads up to. Rather, there are things you are meant to do in different seasons and stages in life. We were all given an individualized assortment of gifts, talents, strengths, and skills, to accomplish what God has purposed for us.

You were created to have a personal relationship with Him, which includes choosing to love Him, being loved by Him, getting to know Him, worshiping Him, and obeying Him. You were created to love His people and take care of His creation. You were created to spread His message and learn His truth. You were created to have a choice to freely accept His gift of salvation or to choose to live apart from Him. He created You to enjoy eternity in His presence. The way each one of us serves, loves, worships, and witnesses, won't look the same but it's all important, meaningful, and beautiful.

Seeds to Plant, Water, and Ruminate:
I was created to experience God's love, freely love Him in return, and show His love to others. I can display this love through worship, obedience, kindness, truth, and using my capabilities (gifts, skills, strengths, and talents) to serve others.

Prayer for Growth

Dear God,

You are my Lord and I am Your servant. Thank You for creating me with a purpose. I'm grateful that I know that my existence is not by chance or accident. Likewise, the universe did not cause itself to come into existence. Let me depend on my Potter to reveal why He has crafted and designed me. Do not allow me to be falsely persuaded by others around me, society, selfish desires, or irrational thinking. Please make it clear to me how my abilities and unique assignments work together to achieve Your purpose for me.

In Jesus' name, I pray. Amen.

Day 7: How Will Using My Gifts, Strengths, and Talents Help Me to Grow?

Growth Scripture:

"Iron sharpens iron, and one person sharpens another."
-Proverbs 27:17 CSB

Growth Insight: Utilizing our spiritual gifts, strengths, skills, and talents, for kingdom purposes, helps us to experience personal and spiritual growth. While serving others, we grow in patience, empathy, gratitude, and humility. There will be times when others may mistreat us, take us for granted, minimize our contributions, ignore us, and criticize us. During these instances, we gain a glimpse into God's perspective when we direct these same actions towards Him. Similarly, we are able to imagine how God may feel when others thank us, appreciate us, respect us, cooperate with us, love us, adhere to our guidance, and welcome us. Serving teaches us to do so without expectation of reward, nor the concern with whether or not others are worthy of our service. Service cultivates a heart of humility, gratitude, and love. We are able to witness God at work in others and within ourselves. The more that we walk in obedience and depend on God's strength, we are better able to recognize the manifestation of His power, mercy, and grace. Dedicating our spiritual gifts, talents, skills, and strengths to God's kingdom brings much maturation, joy, and satisfaction but, it also helps others to grow in their spiritual journey and points them towards God's glory.

Seeds to Plant, Water, and Ruminate:
I love God by loving people. I serve God by serving people. I grow while I help others to grow.

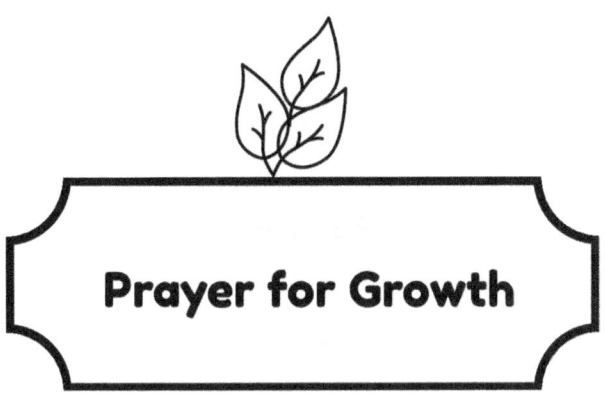

Prayer for Growth

Dear Master,

You deserve all of my praise and worship. As Your servant, I aim to love and serve Your people. Thank You for the gifts, strengths, talents, and skills You have equipped me with in order to serve and fulfill my purpose. Enable me to overcome the obstacles that I will encounter through serving others. Allow me to focus on You instead of the negative aspects of service. Keep my eyes pointed towards Your glory in lieu of my ambitions or inadequacies. Help me to grow and to inspire others to grow in their relationship with You.

I pray these things in Jesus' name, amen.

Step 6: Pray

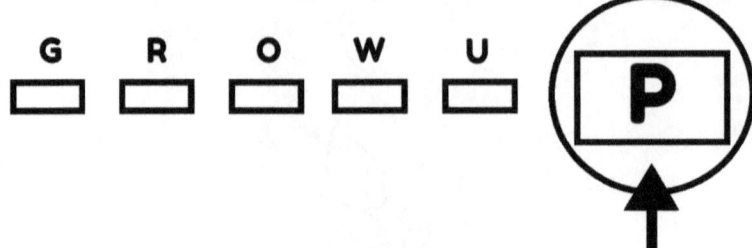

What Is Prayer?

In its simplest form, prayer is communication with God. It is a two-way interaction between us and God, not a mere ritual. During prayer we approach God with a heart of adoration and humility. Prayer involves confession of sins, presenting earnest requests, and offering sincere praise and gratitude. There is an attitude component of prayer. We are not to address God with pridefulness, insincerity, or contempt for Him. Contrarily, we are to present ourselves to God with respect, humbleness, love, and an expectation for Him to act. Prayer is a gift and privilege in and of itself.

Growth Quote:

"Prayer is not getting things from God, that is the most initial stage; prayer is getting into perfect communion with God; I tell Him what I know He knows in order that I may get to know it as He does."
-Oswald Chambers

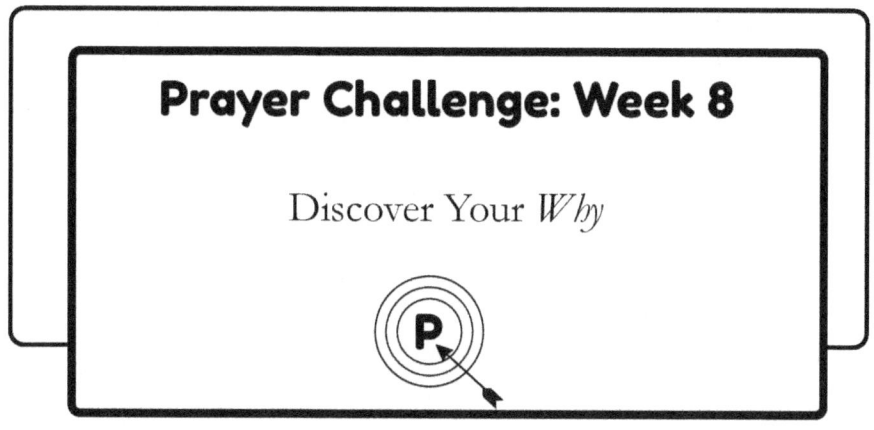

The rationale behind the challenge:

In order to stay motivated, it is important to understand why you are dedicated to prayer. During the times when you are tired, busy, and unmotivated, it may become more challenging to stick to this habit. As a result, it is crucial to remind yourself daily of what you are trying to achieve and how it will deepen your relationship with God. In this week's challenge, you will begin to explore and develop your own personalized reasons to commit to a consistent, daily habit of prayer.

Growth Quote:

"Prayer cleanses from sin, drives away temptations, stamps out persecutions, comforts the fainthearted, gives new strength to the courageous, brings travelers safely home, calms the waves, confounds robbers, feeds the poor, overrules the rich, lifts up the fallen, supports those who are falling, sustains those who stand firm."
-*Tertullian*

Day 1: Why Should I Pray? Part 1

Growth Scripture:

"This is the confidence which we have before Him, that, if we ask anything according to His will, He hears us."
-1 John 5:14 NASB

Growth Insight 1: Prayer is our opportunity to share our hearts with God, thank Him for what He has done in our lives, intervene on the behalf of someone else, seek direction regarding what actions to take, and to make our requests known to God. This is a time when we can be completely vulnerable and transparent. God is our only true safe place. There is no need to hide who we really are because He already knows our inadequacies, sins, failures, struggles, and needs. God's love for us won't be shaken by our shortcomings or openness with Him. In fact, God wants us to bring our broken pieces to Him so He can remold us into something remarkable. We can show God reverence while also being comforted and wrapped in His arms. Prayer is fuel for our souls and nutrition for our spiritual growth. It is a privilege and a loving gift that is a tremendously intimate and transformative experience with our Lord and Savior. God is able and willing to aid, resolve, heal, provide, guide, and protect but we must come to Him humbly and expectantly.

Seeds to Plant, Water, and Ruminate:
Whether I pray for myself or others, He hears me, gives me direction, and knows my heart.

Prayer for Growth

Dear Lord,

I thank You for granting me the privilege to share my heart with You. You listen whether I am angry, heartbroken, confused, grateful, or elated. You give me direction when I am lost, wisdom when I am uncertain, and peace when I am overwhelmed. Thank You for hearing me and answering me. Help me to listen to Your voice and to follow Your instructions.

I pray these things in Jesus' name, amen.

Day 2: Why Should I Pray? Part 2

Growth Scripture:

"If you need wisdom, ask our generous God, and he will give it to you. He will not rebuke you for asking."
-James 1:5 NLT

Growth Insight 2: We all need guidance. Thankfully, we serve an omniscient God who gives wisdom freely and liberally. When you enter prayer with an open mind and heart, there will likely be a significant shift in your attitude, emotions, and/or perspective by its conclusion. During prayer, you may also experience peace, acceptance, comfort, gratitude, joy, and healing. Prayer grants you the strength to resist temptation, patience, and the ability to endure your situation. It brings clarity on His Word and the knowledge to know how to apply His Word. Furthermore, prayer reminds you that you are not alone or aidless, in the hardships of life, and that you are accountable to an authority higher than yourself and the world. Prayer is where you receive the reassurance of your salvation and the confidence to fulfill the purpose and missions God created you to carry out. Prayer works and makes a powerful difference. Take advantage of this gift God has afforded you.

Seeds to Plant, Water, and Ruminate:
Things happen when I pray. When I pray, I can receive peace, strength, and clarity.

Prayer for Growth

Dear Wise and Merciful God,

Thank You for comfort and peace. Thank You for Your patience with me. I come before You today to ask for the wisdom to understand Your Word and the knowledge to know how to apply it to this area I am struggling with right now. Please grant me the strength to endure my current situation. Even when I feel distant from You, I know You are always with me.

I pray these things in Jesus' name, amen.

Day 3: Why Should I Pray? Part 3

Growth Scripture:

"And she made this vow: 'O LORD of Heaven's Armies, if you will look upon my sorrow and answer my prayer and give me a son, then I will give him back to you. He will be yours for his entire lifetime, and as a sign that he has been dedicated to the LORD, his hair will never be cut.'"
-1 Samual 1:11 NLT

Growth Insight 3: Jesus and many other godly figures prayed; we should follow their examples. In the Scriptures, Jesus withdrew to a place of solitude to pray many times. He prayed for our salvation, healing of others, and for His own strength to endure. Praying enabled Jesus to perform countless miracles and bring salvation through His death and resurrection. Hezekiah prayed for healing and deliverance. Subsequently, God delayed the conquering of the nation and extended Hezekiah's life by fifteen years. Hannah and Rachel prayed for a child, which resulted in the births of one of the greatest prophets in history and a ruler who saved his family and Egypt from starvation. David fought many battles, experienced a multitude of victories, fled for his life, and succumbed to temptation. Consequently, he repented, trusted God, worshiped God through song and dance, and prayed for protection and forgiveness. David's sincere actions resulted in him being called a man after God's own heart. These godly individuals understood the need for, and importance of, prayer and were also empowered and utilized through its power.

Seeds to Plant, Water, and Ruminate:
People in the Bible renewed their faith and strength through prayer; I can too.

Prayer for Growth

Dear God in Heaven,

Who sits on the throne of grace, thank You for giving us so many examples of prayer in Your Word. I thank You for the recorded triumphs, struggles, and failures of the saints that came before me. Help me to learn from them and receive encouragement from their stories and Your revelations. Holy Spirit, help me to stay diligent in prayer and intercede when I struggle to know what to say.

I pray these things in Jesus' name, amen.

Day 4: What Happens When I Don't Pray? Part 1

Growth Scripture:

"Come to me, all you who are weary and burdened, and I will give you rest."
-Matthew 11:28 NLT

Growth Insight 1: By not praying, we miss opportunities to express our thankfulness and receive God's assistance. God is owed and deserving of our gratitude. When we do not pray, the opportunity to gain clarity regarding confusion and to experience alleviation from our sorrows is also forfeited. Don't give away your peace, power, and truth by not praying. Receive God's rest and allow Him to ease the burdens you bear. Additionally, don't miss a chance to pray for your loved one's mental and physical wellbeing, relationships, and spiritual journey. Prayer is a wonderful act of service and a beautiful display of love for others.

Seeds to Water and Ruminate:
Life is unnecessarily harder when I do not talk to God every day.

Prayer for Growth

Dear God of Peace,

Thank You for Your ever-present help. Thank You for Your patience with me. I often struggle giving my problems over to You and try to solve them alone. I use my own reasoning instead of seeking Your truth, which leads to confusion. Sometimes I neglect praying for others as frequently as I ought to. Help me to surrender my pride and will to You. Increase my dependency on You and decrease dependency on my own willpower and justifications.

In Jesus' name, amen.

Day 5: What Happens When I Don't Pray? Part 2

Growth Scripture:

"Come close to God, and God will come close to you. Wash your hands, you sinners; purify your hearts, for your loyalty is divided between God and the world."
-James 4:8 NLT

Growth Insight 2: The lack of prayer hinders true intimacy with God. A healthy and flourishing relationship cannot endure or continue to grow without frequent communication. Its growth will be stunted and will eventually wither away. When we do not pray, we are less likely to feel connected to God, have passion for Him, or know His will for our lives. Furthermore, when we deeply love someone, we crave contact with that person and want to truly know them. The more we know God, the more we will love Him and yearn to hear His voice. Without prayer, we often feel alone in circumstances or abandoned by God. If we are not connected to God, it is easy to misinterpret the things that transpire in our daily lives. When we fail to consistently slow down, open our minds, humble our hearts, and go to God in prayer, we allow other people and things to gradually replace Him as our supreme priority. Prayer is a time when we intentionally focus on God and reflect on His monumental impact in our lives. Without prayer, we lose sight of our mission, God's love for us, and His worthiness of our worship and allegiance. Intimacy with God is such a wonderful gift that we lackadaisically relinquish and miss out on when we forsake prayer.

Seeds to Plant, Water, and Ruminate:
I cannot grow or develop my intimacy with God if I don't have genuine and consistent communication with Him.

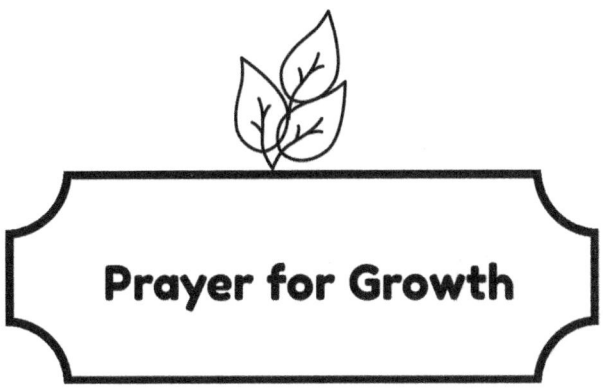

Prayer for Growth

Dear Abba Father,

You are a close and personal God. Thank You for extending an invitation of friendship, parentage, love, grace, mercy, and salvation. I am thankful for being able to speak with You directly and with no need of a mediator, other than Christ. Thank You for remaining near to me even when I am knowingly or unknowingly going astray. I yearn to have a more intimate relationship with You. I want to know You in-depth and experience You in a profound way. Help me to prioritize prayer and to have a longing to converse with You.

In Jesus' name, amen.

Day 6: What Happens When I Don't Pray? Part 3

Growth Scripture:

"When I kept silent about my sin, my body wasted away through my groaning all the day long."
-Psalm 32:3 AMP

Growth Insight 3: When we don't pray, we remain stuck in the same detrimental patterns and make ourselves vulnerable to sin. Consequently, the lack of prayer often makes situations worse and weakens our faith. If we are not brutally honest with God and do not surrender our strongholds to Him, sin will slowly corrode our inner being. We'll live as though we are imprisoned, despite already being set free from sin and suffering. Silence prevents us from sensing God's power and accepting His extended grace, mercy, forgiveness, and deliverance.

It also seems that the less we pray, the more we worry. In the song "What a Friend We Have in Jesus," the writer emphasizes that we often forfeit peace, carry unnecessary burdens, and bear needless pains because we do not take everything to God in prayer. Some people view asking God for help as a weakness. Contrarily, it shows humility, submission, strength, and wisdom. That's exactly the attitude God needs you to have in order to work in your life. Where your pride and willpower end, God's transformation begins.

Seeds to Plant, Water, and Ruminate:
When I keep quiet about my struggles, I leave myself vulnerable to sin, and I forfeit my help and peace.

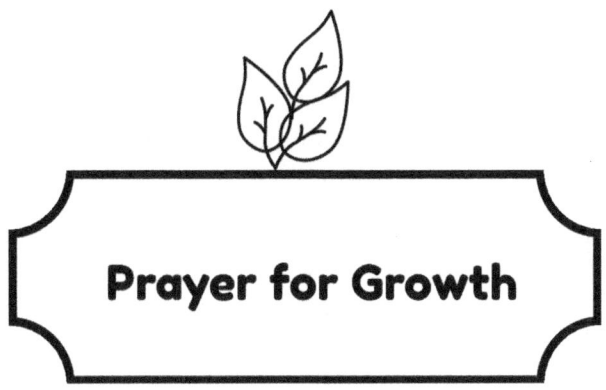

Prayer for Growth

Dear God of Peace,

You are my refuge and my counselor. Thank You for being there with me in times of trouble. You may not always remove me from bad situations or move obstacles out of my way, but You change me in the situation. The Enemy would like for me to suffer in silence so that I feel hopeless and helpless about my circumstances. Please lead me to Your truth, forgive my sins, and strengthen my spirit.

I ask these things in Jesus' name, amen.

Day 7: How Does Prayer Help Me Grow?

Growth Scripture:

"Remain in Me, and I in you. Just as a branch is unable to produce fruit by itself unless it remains on the vine, so neither can you unless you remain in Me. I am the vine; you are the branches. The one who remains in Me and I in him produces much fruit, because you can do nothing without Me."
-John 15:4-5 HCSB

Growth Insight: Prayer assists us in the growth by nourishing all components of our spiritual journey. Prayer keeps all the aspects of your life connected, rooted, and grounded in God. You cannot grow without the intimacy, obedience, reverence, love, and truth that prayer provides. It enables us to keep God as the foremost priority in our lives. With every prayer, we grow in our understanding of God's mercy, our ability to forgive others, and our sense of gratitude. Prayer is also the vessel in which we repent and accept Jesus as Lord and Savior. Praying helps us to obey God's commands and seek His will. Prayer strengthens our belief and elevates our worship. It gives power and effectiveness to our spiritual gifts and talents. Prayer magnifies our faith in God's Word, sovereignty, and salvation. Prayer maintains our spiritual health so that we have the clarity and empowerment that we need to carry out our God-given purpose.

Seeds to Water and Ruminate:
My faith will die if I do not stay rooted in God through prayer.

Prayer for Growth

Dear Heavenly Father,

You are holy and reign over all creation, yet You desire a personal relationship with me. You are righteous and just; however, You forgive my short comings. Enlighten me to realize that prayer is an essential and foundational element to my relationship to You, and that it should not be neglected or taken for granted. Help me to not forget that prayer is a gift and privilege. Thank You for the abundance of Your seen and unseen blessings.

In Jesus' name, amen.

Prayer Challenge: Week 9

Discover Your *Who* and *Where*

The rationale behind the challenge:

This week's challenge is designed to assist you in prayer preparation. Being proactive regarding our external setting and circumstances improves the likelihood of us following through with prayer. It will be beneficial to ready your prayer environment in advance so that you are not scrambling to find items or a place to pray. Unpreparedness will cut into your prayer time. Consider what things you require for your space, distractions that need to be removed, and how you can ensure that there will be privacy. Additionally, it is advisable to determine whether or not you will pray alone, with a partner, or group. If you require a prayer partner, make sure to have updated contact information and availability. Knowing options of who to pray with and where to pray in advance cultivates a readiness and lifestyle of prayer.

Growth Quote:

"Our prayer must not be self-centered. It must arise not only because we feel our own need as a burden we must lay upon God, but also because we are so bound up in love for our fellow men that we feel their need as acutely as our own. To make intercession for men is the most powerful and practical way in which we can express our love for them."
-John Calvin

Day 1: Who Can Pray?

Growth Scripture:

"Let us therefore come boldly to the throne of grace, that we may obtain mercy and find grace to help in time of need."
-Hebrews 4:16 NKJV

Growth Insight 1: God wants to hear from you! You do not have to have someone pray for you or with you. Don't allow feelings of shame, inadequately, uncertainty, or unworthiness to stop you from praying. You may feel ashamed about some of the things you have done recently or that it has been a long time since God has heard from you. Thus, you might believe that you are unworthy to come before God with your requests. Don't wait any longer. The longer you wait, the harder it gets. Simply approach God with a humble, sincere, and repentant heart and He will hear you.

Seeds to Water and Ruminate:
God is merciful and He wants to hear from me.

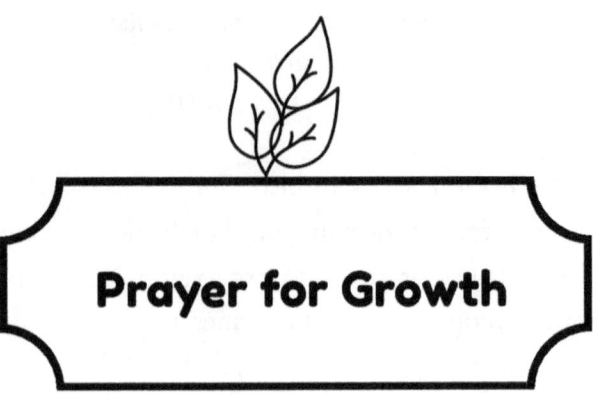

Prayer for Growth

Dear Lord,

Thank You for granting me new mercies and grace each day. I am thankful that Your love is overflowing and that it reaches me. Please help me to see past my shame, guilt, and flaws so that I am able to focus on You and Your love for me. Help me to remain humble so that I seek to understand Your will for my life and not my own selfish desires. Thank You for Your sacrifice on the cross for my sins.

I pray these things in Jesus' name, amen.

Day 2: Who Do I Pray With?

Growth Scripture:

"Again, [amen,] I say to you, if two of you agree on earth about anything for which they are to pray, it shall be granted to them by my heavenly Father. For where two or three are gathered together in my name, there am I in the midst of them."
-Matthew 18:19-20 NAB

Growth Insight 2: Whether you are a newbie Christian or have been a Christ follower for most of your life, it can be beneficial to have someone pray with you or for you. We were not designed to live life alone. If you are new to prayer, or in a dark time in your life where you cannot pray for yourself, it may be wise to have prayer support from others. Make sure you can trust the individual to be confidential and that the person has a mature relationship with Jesus Christ. Ministers, pastors, priests, rabbis, church elders, small group leaders, close friends, and family may be some good options to pray with or for you.

Seeds to Plant, Water, and Ruminate:
I don't have to bear my burdens alone. Others can pray for me when I need help or can't pray for myself.

Prayer for Growth

Dear Lord,

Thank You for the godly people you have placed in my life. Even though I feel alone at times, You have provided me with help. Please give me discernment on who I can trust and go to for prayer.

I ask these things in Jesus' name, amen.

Day 3: Who Do I Pray For?

Growth Scriptures:

"But I say to you, love your enemies, bless those who curse you, do good to those who hate you, and pray for those who spitefully use you and persecute you."
-Matthew 5:44 NKJV

"I urge, then, first of all, that petitions, prayers, intercession and thanksgiving be made for all people— for kings and all those in authority, that we may live peaceful and quiet lives in all godliness and holiness."
-1 Timothy 2:1-2 NIV

Growth Insight: Everyone needs prayer—even the people you don't like and the people who have wronged you. Jesus makes it clear that we should pray not just for the people who do good towards us, but also for our enemies. Pray for the boss that mistreats you or undervalues you. Pray for the spouse that betrayed you or the friend who stole from you. Pray for the children who don't express gratitude or respect. Pray for the teacher who flunked you. Pray for the parent who doesn't understand or support you. Pray for the person who abused or abandoned you. Pray for church leaders and government officials so that they make wise and just decisions. Pray for the needy, sick, and the grieving. Pray for non-believers so that they may learn the truth of God's Word and experience God's love and forgiveness. No one is off limits or not in need of prayer.

Seeds to Plant, Water, and Ruminate:
I should pray for all people regardless of whether I believe they are deserving or not.

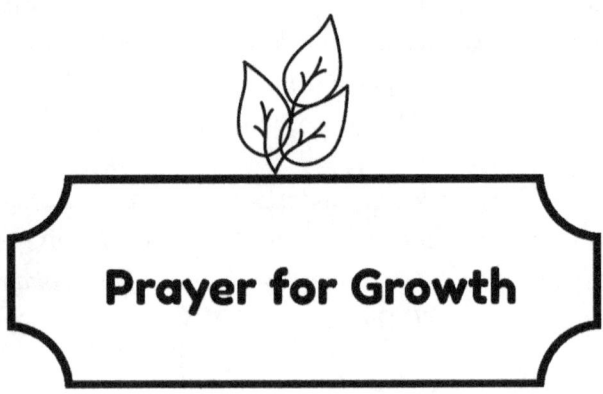

Prayer for Growth

Dear Gracious Lord,

Thank You for Your mercy and lovingkindness. It is difficult for me to pray for those who have hurt me, attempted to harm me, campaigned against me, or caused pain in my life. Enable me to pray for You to work on their hearts. Help me to heal and to not be resentful, judgmental, or vengeful. Remind me that I have also done things that are unworthy of forgiveness, but You have forgiven me. Thank You for Your forgiveness and salvation.

I ask these things in Jesus' name, amen.

Day 4: Who Do I Pray To?

Growth Scripture:

"After this manner therefore pray ye: Our Father which art in heaven, Hallowed be thy name. Thy kingdom come. Thy will be done in earth, as it is in heaven. Give us this day our daily bread. And forgive us our debts, as we forgive our debtors. And lead us not into temptation, but deliver us from evil: For thine is the kingdom, and the power, and the glory, for ever. Amen."
-Matthew 6:9-13 KJV

Growth Insight: We serve one God who is triune: The Father, Son, and Holy Spirit. That is, one being and one nature, yet three distinct persons. Therefore, in theory, if you pray to any person of the Trinity, it's all inclusive. However, there are several instances in the Scriptures where Jesus instructs His disciples to pray to God, the Father. Jesus stipulates that when we do so, we should pray in His name. There are numerous names for God used in the Bible that defines His attributes. You can use any of these names when you address God in your prayers. Jesus also informs His followers that He would send the Holy Spirit to them to help them pray and intercede for them. We pray to the Father, in Jesus' name, through empowerment from the Holy Spirit.

Seeds to Plant, Water, and Ruminate:
When I pray to the Father, I am praying to the Triune God—the Trinity, the Godhead. God the Father, Jesus the Son, and the Holy Spirit are one.

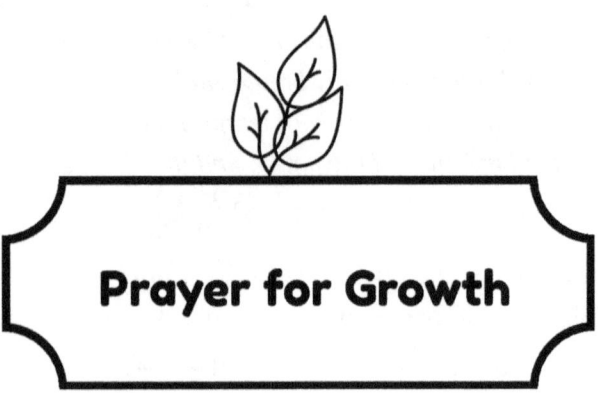

Prayer for Growth

Dear Heavenly Father,

Please teach me how to pray. I want to please You and honor You with my words and actions. Help me to understand who You are and the magnitude of Your power and majesty. Cleanse me of my sins. Thank You for allowing me to have a personal relationship with You.

In Jesus' name, amen.

Day 5: Where Can I Pray?

Growth Scripture:

"But Jesus Himself would often slip away to the wilderness and pray [in seclusion]."
-Luke 5:16 AMP

Growth Insight 1: You can pray wherever you need to: your car, workplace, bedroom, local park, bathroom stall, jail cell, classroom, closet, hospital, store, church, chapel, porch, friend's house, and more. Some people, like Jesus, may prefer to pray in a solitude, private, or quiet place. This option allows you to soley focus on God, without interruptions or distractions, and is usually planned in advance. Whereas others may need to also pray in the midst of a stressful circumstance, chaotic situation, or crisis, which could occur at any time or place. As long as you are not being advertently conspicuous, boastful, or disruptive, it can be a good practice to pray wherever you go. Whether spontaneous or predetermined, anywhere can become a place of fruitful prayer.

Seeds to Plant, Water, and Ruminate:
I need to consider where I can pray ahead of time so that I don't miss a needed opportunity to pray to God.

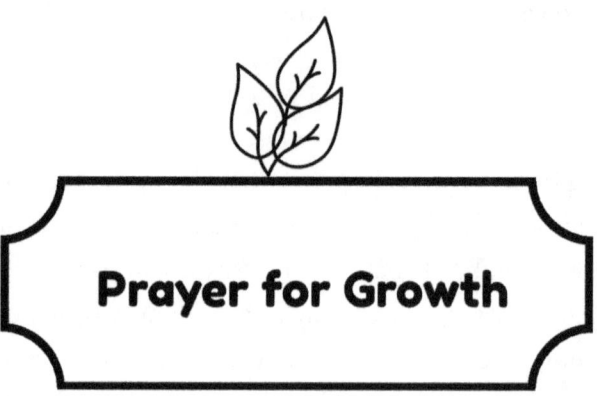

Prayer for Growth

Dear Lord,

Help me to find places where I can fully concentrate on You and receive what You desire to communicate to me. I want to please You and grow in my relationship with You. Thank You for the gift of prayer and access to You.

I ask these things in Jesus' name, amen.

Day 6: Where Is God?

Growth Scriptures:

"And you will seek Me and find Me, when you search for Me with all your heart."
-Jeremiah 29:13 NKJV

"Where can I go from Your Spirit? Or where can I flee from Your presence? If I ascend to heaven, You are there; If I make my bed in Sheol (the nether world, the place of the dead), behold, You are there. If I take wings of the dawn, If I dwell in the remotest part of the sea, Even there Your hand will lead me, and Your right hand will take hold of me."
-Psalm 139:7-10 AMP

Growth Insight: God was in the blazing furnace with Shadrach, Meshach, and Abednego (Daniel 3). God was in the den of lions with Daniel (Daniel 6). Jesus was on the cross next to the repentant thief (Luke 23). God was in the still, small voice to encourage Elijah (1Kings 19). God walked Adam and Eve in the Garden of Eden. God was in the burning bush when He called Moses to become a prophet (Exodus 3). God was in the battle when Gideon's 300 men were outnumbered (Judges 7). The presence of God is evident in creation (Romans 1). The Holy Spirit was there to help Elijah outrun the chariot when Ahab sought to kill him (1Kings 18). God reigns in heaven (Isaiah 66). Jesus sent the Holy Spirit to dwell inside every believer (John 14). God is everywhere, which means that you can seek and find God anywhere.

Seeds to Plant, Water, and Ruminate:
God is always with me no matter the place or situation.

Prayer for Growth

Dear Omnipresent God,

There is no place I can be where You are not there. Thank You for your ever-present help and presence. Thank You for being an active God and not one who is unconcerned about Your people. Help me to feel Your presence when I have put up walls around my heart, gone astray, or have been weighed down by the burdens of this life.

I pray these things in Jesus' name, amen.

Day 7: How Do I Create a Prayer Space?

Growth Scripture:

"But when you pray, go away by yourself, shut the door behind you, and pray to your Father in private. Then your Father, who sees everything, will reward you."
-*Matthew 6:6 NLT*

Growth Insight: The purpose of creating a prayer space is to have an environment that is conducive to focusing on God, feeling His presence, genuinely dialoging with Him, being open to receive what God is trying to convey to you, and personal reflection. You may want to clean out a space or room, check to see when no one will occupy the area, add some candles or aromas, put some cushions down, adjust the lighting, add religious artwork, remove distractions, or add anything else that will set a reverent and reflective mood. Decide whether you need silence, background music, or a white noise machine. Make sure you have all the materials you will need before you begin. For example, you may need your prayer journal, pens, highlighters, bookmarks, eyeglasses, Bible, or a devotional. Create a prayer space that is as comfortable and pleasant as you can make it so that you are eager to return and able to spend adequate time there.

Seeds to Plant, Water, and Ruminate:
Prepping my prayer space will save me time and set the tone for peace and full concentration on God.

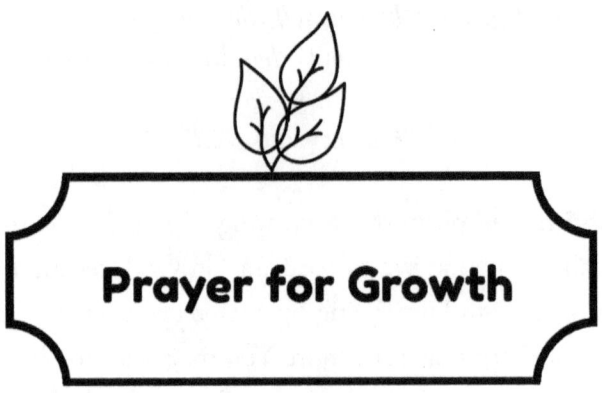

Prayer for Growth

Dear Heavenly Father,

Thank You for Your many blessings. Please help me to find a space that is conducive to personal reflection and allows me to focus on You. I want to feel Your presence and hear from You. Help me to listen with an open and obedient heart.

In Jesus' name, amen.

The rationale behind the challenge:

The goal of this challenge is to explore ways in which you can increase the frequency of your prayers through simple and practical ways. Establishing when to pray helps ensure that praying will take place within your day. This week we will review how prayer can be incorporated into everyday activities making it easier to turn into a daily habit and to produce efficient use of time. During this week, we will also examine how often, and under what circumstances, some of the most prominent biblical figures prayed. As you read through these accounts, it will become apparent that prayers can be offered at any time throughout the day and not just confined to church service, saying grace, or bedtime. The more you pray, the more you are in connection with your Heavenly Father and His will. Connection fertilizes our spiritual growth.

Growth Quote:

"If I fail to spend two hours in prayer each morning, the devil gets the victory through the day. I have so much business, I cannot get on without spending three hours daily in prayer."
-Martin Luther

Day 1: How Often Should I Pray?

Growth Scripture:

"When Daniel learned that the document had been signed, he went into his house. The windows in its upstairs room opened toward Jerusalem, and three times a day he got down on his knees, prayed, and gave thanks to his God, just as he had done before."
-Daniel 6:10 CSB

Growth Insight: Pray daily! In the time of Jesus, it was Jewish tradition to pray three times per day: 9am, 12pm, and 3pm. However, there are examples of Jesus and other biblical figures also praying outside the boundaries of the hours of prayer. Jesus prayed before He healed people, before meals, before miracles, before He was arrested, and on the cross. Jehoshaphat and Deborah prayed before they entered battles. Jacob prayed as he was in fear of his life due to Esau approaching him with armed men. The number of times you pray per day depends on how often you want to express your gratitude and homage, ask for God's help to refrain from sin, seek His aid and guidance, or feel His presence.

Seeds to Plant, Water, and Ruminate:
I can talk to God an infinite number of times per day. He is always available.

Prayer for Growth

Dear Omnipresent and Omnipotent God,

Thank You for Your grace and mercy. Thank You for help when I am in need. Thank You for granting me access to communicate with You. Help me to remember that I need to be in constant communication with You in order to focus on Your truth and positivity instead of the negative messages of the world and the chaos all around me. Let Your love drive out my fears and concerns and replace it with Your peace and glory.

In Jesus' name, amen.

Day 2: What If I Only Pray When It's My Last Resort?

Growth Scripture:

"Rejoice always, pray without ceasing, give thanks in all circumstances; for this is the will of God in Christ Jesus for you."
-1 Thessalonians 5:16-18 ESV

Growth Insight: Prayer is not designed to be your last resort. It should be your first inclination and action. Don't wait until you have exhausted every option, and your life is in shambles before you pray about a situation. Be proactive and pray about every aspect of your life before something goes wrong or before you have to make a decision. Sometimes pride gets in our way, and we feel that we should handle things all on our own. Prayer is not a sign of weakness. Prayer is a sign of obedience and relationship with your Heavenly Father. Other times we feel as though we are bothering God with our lowly problems while there are more severe issues going on in the world. God doesn't use a measuring stick to determine if your prayer is too insignificant or too substantial to answer. God cares about you and your wellbeing. After all, the things that you feel are too minor or too major to pray about now will become more severe the longer you wait.

Seeds to Plant, Water, and Ruminate:
My Heavenly Father wants to hear from me whether my issues are big or small. He wants to speak with me even when there is nothing wrong at all.

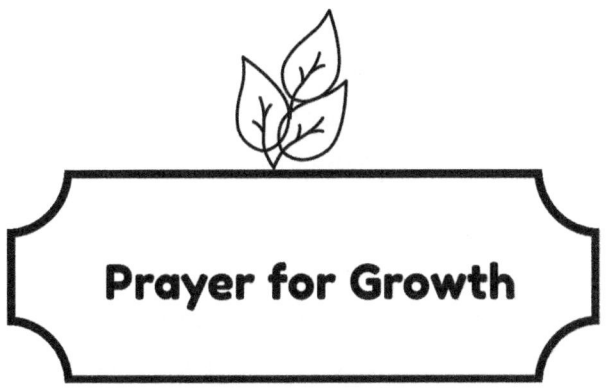

Prayer for Growth

Dear Heavenly Father,

You are ruler over all matters and creation. Thank You for Your love and care for me. Thank You for the many things You have entrusted with me. Help me to have no reservations about speaking with You. Please remove any fear, guilt, shame, pride, or insecurities that would prevent me from consulting with You. Remind me that You are a generous, gracious, and merciful God.

I ask these things in Jesus' name, amen.

Day 3: How Can I Find More Time to Pray? Part 1

Growth Scripture:

"One day Peter and John were going up to the temple at the time of prayer —at three in the afternoon."
-Acts 3:1 CSB

Growth Insight 1: Put prayer on your daily schedule because it won't just happen organically. Designate a specific time that you will stop and pray. We often think that we can just squeeze prayer in at some point of the day—when we have time. However, something always seems to come up and we keep pushing it back. Before we know it, the day is over, and we have yet to pray. Then at the end of the day, we are too tired or rushed to have a true meaningful and reflective prayer experience.

Scheduling prayer helps to create and maintain a consistent prayer life. It is important to allocate a realistic amount of time and quantity. Additionally, try to avoid scheduling prayer near activities that often run over their allotted time and encroach on your designated prayer time. Be careful not to become so regimented that you only pray according to your daily organizer. Spontaneous prayer can be so rewarding, healing, and nourishing to the soul. Scheduling prayer merely serves as a tool to ensure that prayer remains a priority and that it occurs frequently and on a daily basis. Remember that things happen that are out of your control. If you miss your intended prayer goal one day, make your needed adjustments and start fresh the next day. Be kind to yourself. Don't become discouraged, and don't throw your entire plan away. God's mercies are new every morning. Try again tomorrow, and keep in mind that you are already further ahead than you were yesterday.

Seeds to Plant, Water, and Ruminate:
I have to be consistent and intentional about prayer.

Prayer for Growth

Dear Lord,

Help me to designate time to converse with You throughout the day. Help me to remember that time with You is sacred and necessary. You are deserving of respect and honor. I thank You for allowing me to be of sound mind and able to pray. Help me to be consistent and intentional about scheduling time to pray.

In Jesus' name, amen.

Day 4: How Can I Find More Time to Pray? Part 2

Growth Scripture:

"Making the most of your time, because the days are evil. Therefore, do not be foolish, but understand what the Lord's will is."
-Ephesians 5:16-17 NASB

Growth Insight 2: In order to find more time to pray, you can shorten the amount of time you spend scrolling social media, playing games, or watching tv. It is easy to go down the rabbit hole as we click from one post or article to another. We tell ourselves that we are going to respond to just one more social media post, email, or text message. There is just one more round we must conquer on our mobile, video, or computer game. One episode or video can turn into an entire binge-watching event. Instead of one last late-night scroll session or the midafternoon technology-filled slump break, five to fifteen minutes of prayer can go a long way.

Seeds to Plant, Water, and Ruminate:
Time spent with God is never a waste; it's the best thing I can do with my time.

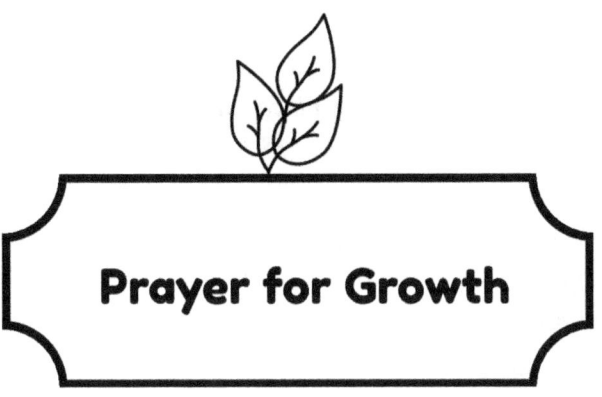

Prayer for Growth

Dear Lord,

I thank You for all the advances in technology that my generation has made. It helps to teach me things, keep me informed, and entertains me. However, help me to not become so consumed by social media, games, and tv that it leaves me minuscule time with You and my family. Lord, please guide me on how to maintain a healthy balance in my life.

In Jesus' name, amen.

Day 5: How Can I Find More Time to Pray? Part 3

Growth Scripture:

"And in the morning, rising up a great while before day, he went out, and departed into a solitary place, and there he prayed."
-Mark 1:35 KJV

Growth Insight 3: Another way to incorporate more prayer time into your day is to adjust your waking hours. If feasible, you can plan to wake up a few minutes earlier or stay up a few minutes later than usual. However, it may be the most beneficial to schedule prayer around a time when you are the most alert. You don't want to fall asleep, be too tired to concentrate, or have too many interruptions. Alternatively, you can take some time out of your lunch break, study hall, or during the kids' nap time to pray. While in your car (or other mode of transportation), you can take time to pray before you drive to your destination, before you enter your destination, or before you enter your home. It may seem as though there is too much to do to be able to pray, but the truth is that prayer lightens the load. Prayer makes life feel more manageable.

Seeds to Plant, Water, and Ruminate:
Life seems busier, more exhausting, and more difficult when I don't pray.

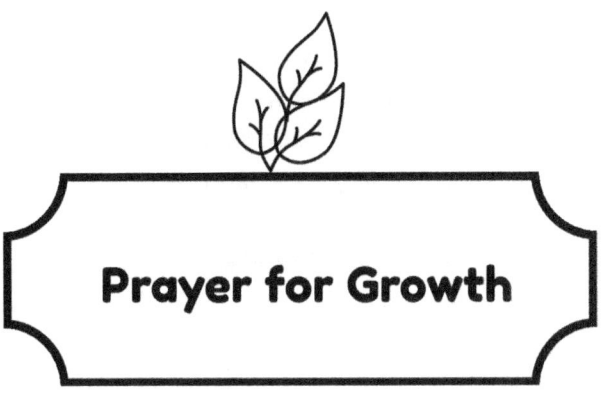

Prayer for Growth

Dear God,

Thank You for the emotional rest You provide for me. Help me to take refuge and delight in our communication. Aid me making prayer a priority in my life. Remind me that You want to hear from me and that prayer is vital to our relationship. I give You glory, honor, and praise.

In Jesus' name, amen.

Day 6: How Can I Find More Time to Pray? Part 4

Growth Scripture:

"Again I say to you, if two of you agree on earth about anything they ask, it will be done for them by my Father in heaven. For where two or three are gathered in my name, there am I among them."
-Matthew 18:19-20 ESV

Growth Insight 4: Joining a regularly scheduled prayer group can be helpful in including more prayer into your life. There are churches and individuals that organize daily prayer call-ins and prayer meetings. These calls may be a phone line or a reoccurring video call link. People can submit prayer requests, and the leader prays over the issues right on the call. Other churches and groups of believers may have in-person weekly or monthly prayer groups and prayers services. Prayer group chats through text message are also an option. You can start a prayer group with your friends or establish a prayer partner. Praying with others can aid you in being more comfortable with prayer and enlighten you on how prayer has made a difference in the lives of others. Being accountable to other people can assist you in remaining encouraged and motivated to pray frequently and consistently.

Seeds to Plant, Water, and Ruminate:
Prayer groups and prayer partners can keep me accountable to pray and offer support through all seasons of my life.

Prayer for Growth

Dear God of the Universe and of Angel Armies,

Thank You for Your presence in my life. Please direct me to a group of fellow believers who can pray for me. Help me to also be a blessing to them by improving my prayer life and faith. Provide me with insight on how to pray for my fellow brothers and sisters in Christ.

In Jesus' name, amen.

Day 7: How Can I Find More Time to Pray? Part 5

Growth Scripture:

"I will bless the LORD at all times; his praise shall continually be in my mouth."
-Psalm 34:1 ESV

Growth Insight 5: Prayer can enhance some of the activities that are a part of your daily routine. You can incorporate prayer into tasks that you already engage in. For example, you might pray while walking in the park, doing yoga, undergoing medical treatment (e.g., dialysis or chemotherapy), Bible crafting, doing chores, relaxing in a bubble bath, reading the Psalms, meditating on a Bible verse, journaling about a prayer topic, or sketching a Bible theme. It is okay to talk to God throughout the day and while you do ordinary things. Any hour or circumstance is acceptable to give thanks to our Lord or to call on Him for aid.

Seeds to Plant, Water, and Ruminate:
I can talk to God all day long.

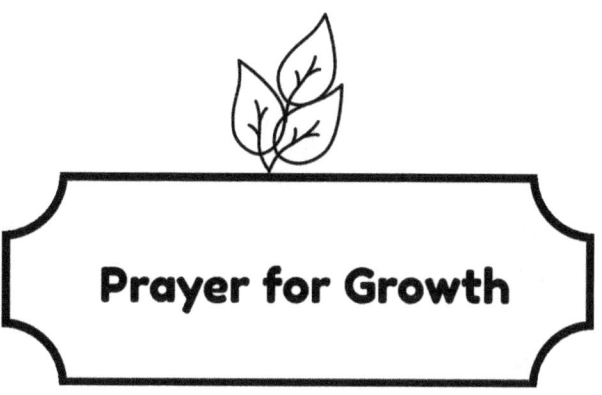

Prayer for Growth

Dear God,

I want to spend more time in Your presence. I want to hear from You and feel close to You. I desire to experience Your peace, influence, and protection all day long. Thank You for the gift of the Holy Spirit who is always present with me. Help me to allow the Spirit to direct my path and to purify my mind. Guide me so that You remain as my top priority.

In Jesus' name, amen.

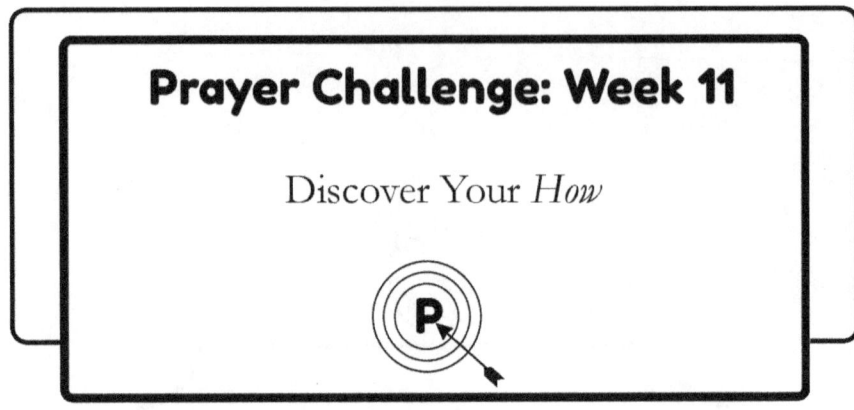

Prayer Challenge: Week 11

Discover Your *How*

The rationale behind the challenge:

This week's challenge is intended to foster comfortability with prayer and to provide some optional structure suggestions. The feeling of not knowing how to pray can be a discouraging barrier that deters many from beginning to pray. A sense of knowing how to carry out a task makes most of us feel more comfortable, confident, and motivated to complete it. The good news is that there is no pass/fail prayer test. You are not wrong if you use a prayer formula or just speak unscripted from the heart. Many people find a formula to be helpful guidance or a good starting point until they become more at ease with praying. The most important aspect of prayer is to beseech God respectively, genuinely, and humbly, not to master a script or structure.

Growth Quote:

"Pray until you can pray; pray to be helped to pray and do not give up praying because you cannot pray. For it is when you think you cannot pray that is when you are praying."
-Charles Spurgeon

Day 1: Is There a Correct Way to Pray?

Growth Scriptures:

"Therefore, I want the men in every place to pray, lifting up holy hands without anger or argument."
-1 Timothy 2:8 HCSB

"Now Hannah spoke in her heart; only her lips moved, but her voice was not heard."
-1 Samual 1:13 NKJV

Growth Insight: The Bible does not provide us with a sequence of prayer rituals that we must adhere to every time we pray. Neither are we commanded to fold our hands, get down on our knees, raise up our hands, lie prostrate on the floor, stand up, bow our heads, close our eyes, vocalize words, or internalize prayer. However, there are ample examples of different believers in the Bible utilizing most of these prayerful acts of worship. Many people observe these practices out of reverence for God's holiness and as a symbol of surrender to Him. These gestures are to serve as an outward reflection of our inner humility and focus on God.

Seeds to Plant, Water, and Ruminate:
My prayer gestures should be done out of reverence and honor for God, not for show.

Prayer for Growth

Dear Lord,

You are a holy and all-powerful God. Help me to appreciate the scope of Your majesty. I pray that my actions reverence and honor You. Purify my heart so that it is acceptable to You. Thank You for Your presence in my life.

In Jesus' name, amen.

Day 2: Do I Need a Prayer Formula?

Growth Scripture:

"And pray in the Spirit on all occasions with all kinds of prayers and requests. With this in mind, be alert and always keep on praying for all the Lord's people."
-Ephesians 6:18 NIV

Growth Insight: We are not required to use a specific prayer formula or scripted prayer in order to approach God in prayer. When Jesus' disciples asked Him how to pray, Jesus used the Lord's Prayer (Matthew 6:9-13) as one example. However, Jesus, prophets, judges, apostles, kings, and other believers in the Bible use a variety of different prayer structures. There is no specific format believers are commanded to utilize for every prayer time. Moreover, many prayers in the Bible do have commonalities in it such as giving praise and thanks to God and making requests on the behalf of self and others. Different occasions necessitate different prayers.

Seeds to Plant, Water, and Ruminate:
I can pray to God in a way that gives Him respect and honor without the use of a prayer formula.

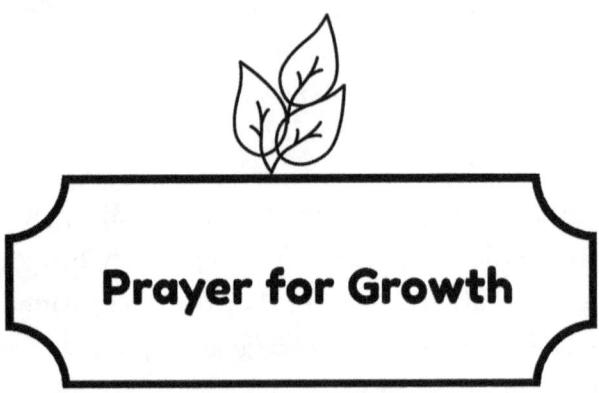

Prayer for Growth

Dear Heavenly Father,

Please teach me how to pray. I want to bring glory and honor to Your name. I want to hear from You and be able to express my thoughts and feelings to You. Thank You for Your faithfulness and mercy.

In Jesus' name, amen.

Day 3: How Do I Use Prayer Formulas? Part 1

Growth Scripture:

"I call on You, God, because You will answer me; listen closely to me; hear what I say."
-Psalm 17:6 HCSB

Prayer Model 1: The A.C.T.S. Prayer Model is widely used among many Christian denominations. This model consists of four parts:

1. **Adoration:** In this section, we praise God for who He is, not for what He has done. You can include different names of God or His attributes, such as Heavenly Father, Lord, Almighty, Promise Keeper, Faithful One, Healer, Savior, Comforter, Holy One, or Way Maker. Make this part personal to who God has been to you.
2. **Confession:** Here, we confess our sins and ask for God's forgiveness.
3. **Thanksgiving:** In this section, we thank God for what He has done for us.
4. **Supplication:** Finally, this is where we make requests to God on behalf of ourselves and others.

Seeds to Plant, Water, and Ruminate:
I can use a prayer model as a guide, to get me started in my prayer life, but I can also just speak to God from my heart.

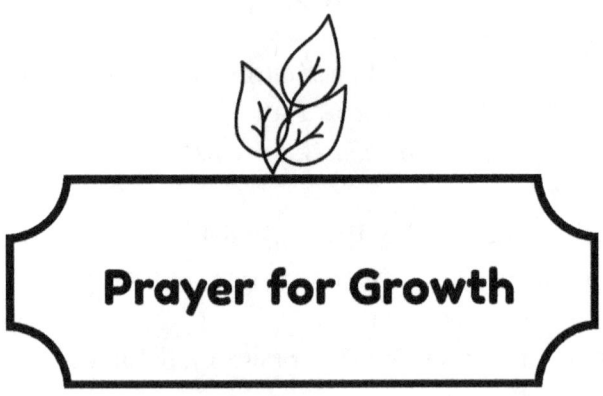

Prayer for Growth

(Adoration) Dear Lord,

You are holy, almighty, and merciful. You keep Your promises and are faithful towards me. **(Confession)** Please forgive me for my disobedience to Your Word, my doubts, and the unforgiveness I have in my heart. **(Thanksgiving)** Thank You for extending Your grace to me and for saving me. Thank You for giving me purpose, peace, and direction. Thank You for healing and Your unconditional love. **(Supplication)** Lord, please help me serve others in the way You have equipped me to do. I ask for protection and provision for my family. Please keep our country at peace with other nations and restore our country to be a God-fearing nation once more.

In Jesus' name, I pray. Amen.

Day 4: How Do I Use Prayer Formulas? Part 2

Growth Scripture:

"For this reason also, since the day we heard this, we haven't stopped praying for you. We are asking that you may be filled with the knowledge of His will in all wisdom and spiritual understanding."
-Colossians 1:9 HCSB

Prayer Model 2: The Five Finger Prayer assists us in remembering who we are to pray for. It is often used as a visual aid for children but is a wonderful guide for adults as well. The thumb represents close friends and family. The index finger is a symbol for the individuals who give us instruction and healing, such as teachers, clergy, and medical professionals. The tallest (i.e., middle) finger is representative of those who *stand tall* for us such as military, government, and law enforcement. The ring finger is for those who are sick, needy, or troubled. The little finger represents yourself. Remember to pray for both yourself and others.

Seeds to Plant, Water, and Ruminate:
Praying for myself and others is pleasing to God. My prayers make a difference.

Prayer for Growth

Dear Lord,

Help me to not just think of my needs when I pray. Likewise, remind me that it is not selfish to also pray for myself. Thank You for the individuals that have aided me in my life and who have prayed for me. Help me to see how prayer has impacted my life and the lives of others. Thank You for graciously gifting me with the power of prayer.

In Jesus' name, amen.

Day 5: How Long Should I Pray?

Growth Scripture:

"And when you pray, do not keep on babbling like pagans, for they think they will be heard because of their many words. Do not be like them, for your Father knows what you need before you ask him."
-Matthew 6:8 NIV

Growth Insight: Your prayer should be as long as it needs to be. It should not be rushed or prolonged just to add fluff. The length of your prayer will depend on the number of issues you need to pray about, the direness of the situation, time restraints, and your emotional state at the time. For example, if a person is being confrontational with you, you may need to say a quick, in-the-moment prayer for the ability to restrain yourself and to ask for wisdom, grace, and empathy. If you are grieving or in emotional distress, you many need to pray all night to be comforted. Jesus prayed all night for those He had come to save and for His strength to endure the agony of the cross. Whether you pray for three minutes or three hours, your prayer should be sincere, and your heart should be open to God.

Seeds to Plant, Water, and Ruminate:
My prayer can be effective regardless of its brevity or length, but I should allow the Spirit to lead me.

Prayer for Growth

Dear Lord,

Open my heart to You during prayer. Help me to have a heart that is receptive to Your guidance. Allow the Holy Spirit to move me to action, conviction, and surrender. Enable me to view things through Your lens. Holy Spirit intercede for me during prayer and aid me in knowing what to pray and for what length of time.

I ask these things in Jesus' name, amen.

Day 6: How Do I Use a Prayer Journal?

Growth Scripture:

"Great are the works of the LORD; they are pondered by all who delight in them."
-Psalm 111:2 NIV

Growth Insight: There are two ways that you can use a prayer journal: freestyle or preselected prompts. A freestyle blank journal allows you to write down prayers to God without any predesignated topics. Writing allows you to slow down, process your thoughts, and analyze the situation more clearly. A prayer journal with prompts provides you with thought provoking questions to reflect upon. Both styles help you to gain insight and a new perspective on the matters you are praying about. Writing can help us express our thoughts and feelings more effectively, and it enables us to focus better on God. It is important to review your prayers at a later date so you can see how God has answered them and recognize how much you have grown in your spiritual journey.

Seeds to Plant, Water, and Ruminate:
Writing helps me to process my thoughts, feelings, motives, and actions, so that I can better see God's truth in my circumstances.

Prayer for Growth

Dear Father in Heaven,

All glory and praise to Your holy name. Let Your will be done. Help me to meditate on Your grace, mercy, and blessings through writing. Allow the Spirit to guide me as I am sometimes left searching for the right words to say. As I look back over my prayers, help me to gain insight into my circumstances, strengthen my faith, and express appreciation to You.

In Jesus' name, amen.

Day 7: Does My Attitude Matter When I Pray?

Growth Scriptures:

"The sacrifices God desires are a humble spirit—O God, a humble and repentant heart you will not reject."
-Psalm 51:17 NET

"Therefore I tell you, all that you ask for in prayer, believe that you will receive it and it shall be yours."
-Mark 11:24 NAB

Growth Insight: During prayer, our attitude matters because God examines our hearts (Jeremiah 17:10). When we approach God with humbleness, reverence, faith, and sincerity, He hears our prayers. We have to trust that God is just, merciful, righteous, and will answer our prayers. God does not honor prayers when they are offered up only for show or when the heart is unrepentant. Prayer must be sincere. God does not entertain prayers when there is disbelief, malicious intentions, or disrespectful undertones. We must have respect for God and an expectation that something will change when we pray.

Seeds to Plant, Water, and Ruminate:
A heart of trust, sincerity, repentance, and humility is pleasing to God.

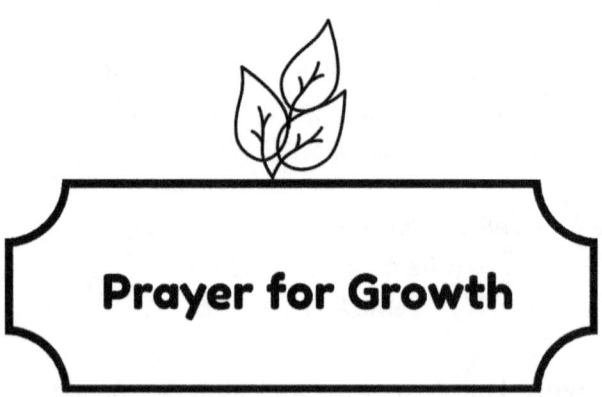

Prayer for Growth

Dear Omniscient and Almighty God,

I praise and honor Your holy name. I come before You with a humble and grateful heart. Please forgive my sins that are known and unknown to me. Please give me a heart and attitude that is pleasing in Your sight. When I am distraught or confused, please protect my heart from bitterness and hopelessness. Help me to remember that Your knowledge and wisdom exceeds my reasoning. Steer me away from pride and arrogance.

I ask these things in Jesus' name, amen.

The rationale behind the challenge:

If God truly is the Lord of our lives, then we must give him control over every area of our lives. So, what should we pray about? The answer is everything. Pray about every aspect of your life; nothing is off limits. God cares about it all! The purpose of this week's challenge is to examine the areas of your life that you've overlooked, avoided, or have not fully surrendered to God's lordship through prayer.

Growth Scripture:

"Don't worry about anything; instead, pray about everything. Tell God what you need, and thank him for all he has done."

-Philippians 4:6 NLT

Day 1: What Do I Pray About?

Part 1: Friends, Family, Significant Others, and Leadership

Growth Scripture:

"For this reason we have always prayed for you, ever since we heard about you. We ask God to fill you with the knowledge of his will, with all the wisdom and understanding that his Spirit gives."
-Colossians 1:9 GNT

Growth Insight: We are privileged to have the gift of intercessory prayer; we can pray on the behalf of others. When our children are having behavioral issues or straying away from God, we can pray for their temperament and return to God. When our friends are brokenhearted or grieving, we can pray for their strength, peace, and comfort. When we are in conflict with our spouse, we can pray for a resolution that brings us closer together instead of driving us apart. Also, when our spouses are going through health problems, identity crises, career crossroads, mental health concerns, or facing challenging obstacles, we can pray for their wisdom, healing, and guidance. The leadership of the country and of churches needs prayer for emotional support and for wisdom in making ethical decisions. Our supervisors need prayer to treat us fairly, not to take us for granted, do their jobs properly, fittingly raise our pay, and to promote us when deserved. God can change the heart of our spouse, parent, friend, child, supervisor, or other relatives when they mistreat us or are in opposition with us. We cannot force others to do what we want or to alter their behavior. However, God can change our own perspective of the person or situation, give us the tools and guidance that we need to move forward, and help us to healthily manage our emotions and responses to the other person.

Seeds to Plant, Water and Ruminate:
When the attitudes and behaviors of others do not change, God can change the way I respond and the way I view their behavior. My new response may change their hearts and actions.

Prayer for Growth

Dear God of Peace and Love,

Help me to display peace and love in my relationships. Give me the wisdom and humility to resolve conflicts without imposing my will or edifying myself. Please enable me to display behavior that is reflective of Christ during resolutions. In the instances when I must exercise grace, change my heart and my view of the circumstances. Help me to humanize those in authority and realize that they need prayer for their mental health, spiritual growth, decision making, personal issues, need for confidants, and compassion just as I do.

In Jesus' name, I pray. Amen.

Day 2: What Do I Pray About?

Part 2: Temptations, Strongholds, and Forgiveness

Growth Scriptures:

"For I do not do the good I want to do. Instead, I keep on doing the evil I do not want to do. So this is the principle I have discovered: When I want to do good, evil is right there with me. For in my inner being I delight in God's law. But I see another law at work in my body, warring against the law of my mind and holding me captive to the law of sin that dwells within me."
-Romans 7:19,21-23 BSB

"Therefore, to keep me from becoming conceited, I am forced to deal with a recurring problem. That problem, Satan's messenger, torments me to keep me from being conceited. I begged the Lord three times to take it away from me."
-2 Corinthians 12:7-8 GW

Growth Insight: In the book of Romans, Paul is describing his constant battle with sin. Paul loves God's laws, and he knows that they are positive and beneficial to him. He wants to follow through on what God has required of him, and of all of us, but in some areas, he is still succumbing to temptation. In 2 Corinthians, Paul confesses that he has an issue that he pleaded to God to remove. However, God did not take away his issue in order that Paul could rely on God's power and not his own strength. It appears that Paul believes that if God would not have done this, his ego would have become inflated, thinking that his own willpower or righteousness had delivered him from the problem.

There are times when we as believers suffer from what is commonly referred to as strongholds. These are sins that have been extremely difficult for us to stop doing. We may have prayed for years about a particular sin or tried to unsuccessfully break the habit on our own. Maybe we haven't prayed to God to remove this desire from us out of fear of what would happen if we were freed from it. Sometimes we erroneously believe that removal of that sin will leave a permanent void in our lives. Strongholds can become crutches that actually harm us instead of helping us. Hence, we should not believe the lie that since we have struggled with a certain sin for so long, God approves or condones it. Be patient. Ask for forgiveness, strength, and assistance while attempting to cease the transgression. God is gracious, willing, and able to help us.

Seeds to Plant, Water, and Ruminate:
Just because God hasn't delivered me from this sin yet doesn't mean that He won't or that He affirms my sin.

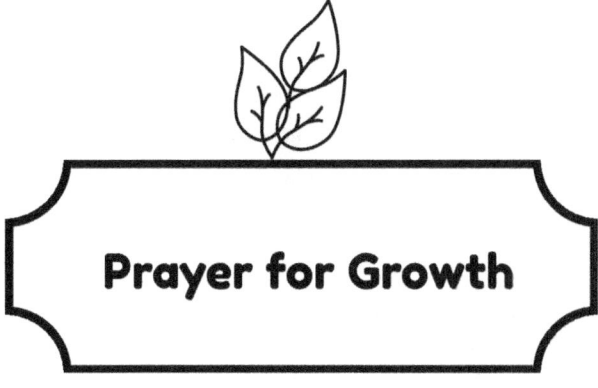

Dear Lord,

Thank You for Your patience and grace. You have the power to break any chain of sin. I have tried, unsuccessfully, for so long to overcome the temptation of this stronghold and fear that it will never dissipate. Please forgive me of this repeated shortcoming. Show me the permanent way out and remove the desire from me.
Guide my feet away from compromising people, places, and situations. Lord, help me to trust that what You can provide to me is better than this sin. Protect my mind against lies that this stronghold is of no consequence, insignificant, good, acceptable, or incurable.

In Jesus' holy and precious name, amen.

Day 3: What Do I Pray About?

Part 3: School, Work, and Ambitions

Growth Scriptures:

"Whoever gives attention to the LORD's word prospers, and blessed is the person who trusts the LORD."
-Proverbs 16:20 GW

"Delight thyself also in Jehovah; And he will give thee the desires of thy heart. Commit thy way unto Jehovah; Trust also in him, and he will bring it to pass."
-Psalm 37:4-5 ASV

Growth Insight: Attending school, going to work, and pursuing our dreams take up a considerable amount of our life. Therefore, we want to make sure that we are making the most out of our time and are in line with God's will for our lives. While attending school, you can pray about learning the knowledge, skills, and discipline needed for your future endeavors. There may also be issues with bullying, teacher discrimination, or uncertainty of which career path to take. You can take all of these concerns to our Heavenly Father.

Once we settle on an occupation or vocation, we face challenges in the work environment. Whether you work at home, from home, or at an organization, we have interactions with others and tasks we must achieve. We can pray for patience, mental and physical strength, conflict resolution skills, time management skills, work-life balance, productivity, and advancement.

In addition to our profession, many of us have passions and dreams that we want to chase after. There is a sense of joy, peace, and satisfaction when we engage in activities that we feel called or destined to do and are passionate about. We can pray that we are able to experience this phenomenon in our lives. Ultimately, the most important thing to pray about is that we are showing the love of God to others, honoring God, and being obedient to God in all that we do and pursue.

Seeds to Plant, Water, and Ruminate:
Whether I am a volunteer, stay-at-home parent, student, homemaker, retiree, or a career professional, my growth and ambitions must be grounded in Christ.

Prayer for Growth

Dear Lord,

You are the Bright and Morning Star. Shine Your light on me and the path that I should walk. Drive my passions and tame my endeavors to bend to Your will. Strengthen my heart when I feel faint in my efforts. Dissolve my doubts when my confidence wanes. Teach me the skills that I am lacking to fulfill what it is You want me to do. Help me to grow so that I can lead others to You no matter the role I'm currently assigned. Remind me that my identity and worth is not depended upon my roles but comes from my identity in You. I pray that I feel satisfied by having the knowledge that You are utilizing me to do great works for Your kingdom.

In Jesus' name, amen.

Day 4: What Do I Pray About?

Part 4: Betrayals and Being Wronged

Growth Scriptures:

"It is of the Lord's mercies that we are not consumed, because his compassions fail not. They are new every morning."
-Lamentations 3:22-23 KJV

"Dearly beloved, avenge not yourselves, but rather give place unto wrath: for it is written, Vengeance is mine: I will repay, saith the Lord."
-Romans 12:19 KJV

Growth Insight: Similarly to grief, experiencing a betrayal, or being wronged, can leave you feeling completely devastated and lost. You may struggle to make sense of your life and not know how to move on. Shame, embarrassment, sadness, worry, and self-blame may also surface. In a marriage relationship, adultery kills the marriage and can leave a family in upheaval. Being wronged by others also takes many forms. For instance, family abandoning you, companies scamming you out of money, co-workers lying on you, managers not promoting you, or friends stealing from you can have a crushing impact as well. In the moment, putting the pieces of your life back together may seem impossible or like an uphill battle. However, we serve a God who can resurrect dead marriages, restore possessions that were taken, build new friendships, and create new opportunities. Prayer can turn situations around and make a way when we don't see a way.

Seeds to Plant, Water, and Ruminate:
My prayers can resurrect dead situations and sculpt a beautiful new creation.

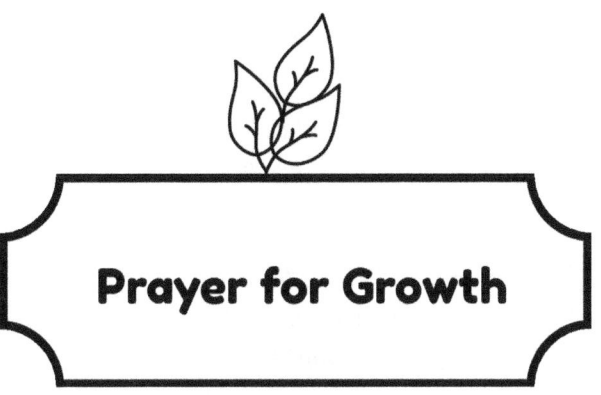

Prayer for Growth

Dear Lord,

You are a God of peace and comfort. Thank You for Your faithfulness, trustworthiness, and honesty while others have betrayed me. You are there to dry my tears in the depths of the night and You lighten the load of my burdens. Ease the suffering that others have caused and heal my heart. Open my eyes to see how You will bring glory and restoration. Remind me that the pain I feel now is being used as fertilizer to activate my growth in faith, wisdom, and character.

I ask all these things in Jesus' name, amen.

Day 5: What Do I Pray About?

Part 5: Finances and Basic Needs

Growth Scriptures:

"I have been young, and now am old; Yet have I not seen the righteous forsaken, Nor his seed begging bread."
-Psalm 37:25 ASV

"But if God thus clothes the grass of the field, existing today and tomorrow being thrown in the furnace, will He not much more clothe you, O you of little faith?"
-Matthew 6:30 BLB

Growth Insight: At the time of this writing, inflation is at an all-time high and the stock market is unsteady. Dollar stores cost more than a dollar and money doesn't stretch far for any product or service. Financial insecurity is the source of stress for millions of people and strains many relationships. Financial hardship can affect where we live, which dreams we put on hold, how many jobs we must work, and how often we can afford needed medical care. It can determine the mode of transportation we use, the nutrition we consume, the clothes we wear, and even the hobbies or family activities we enjoy. It may feel as though we have more needs than resources or more bills than money.

Fortunately, we serve a God of many riches and who has all power in His hands. Jesus reminds His disciples to not worry about their practical needs because God knows our needs before we even pray. God can use that random stranger to pay your bill, send an unexpected check in the mail, create a new job opportunity, or direct you to a church offering free clothes, food, and supplies. He might move someone to offer you a free living space, stir that coworker's heart to give you a ride, and more. You may not know how or when God will act, but you can be certain that He will take care of your needs.

Seeds to Plant, Water, and Ruminate:

My resources may seem limited, but God's wealth is unmeasured. He is able and willing to provide for me.

Prayer for Growth

Dear Yahweh Yireh,

My provider, You have not abandoned me, nor have You ignored my needs. Thank You for providing for me in ways that I have not acknowledged or recognized. Help me to trust You in my times of worry and disbelief. Assist me in having patience as I wait on You to move on my behalf.

In Jesus' name, amen.

Day 6: What Do I Pray About?

Part 6: Gratitude

Growth Scripture:

"Taste and see that the LORD is good. How happy is the man who takes refuge in Him! You who are His holy ones, fear Yahweh, for those who fear Him lack nothing."
-Psalm 34:8-9 HCSB

Growth Insight: Gratitude is the key to authentic internal joy and happiness. It keeps us focused on the goodness of God instead of on ourselves and the circumstances around us. However, we often fail to take time and reflect on the ways God has been generous, merciful, kind, and comforting to us. When things are going well, it's easy to forget the times when he healed us, protected us, forgave us, provided for us, and got us out of trouble. At times, we may take our blessings for granted and even feel entitled to them.

Worries, possessions, ambitions, losses, successes, excursions, failures, relationships, and problems can distract us and distort our view on the need for gratitude. When we experience things such as grief, sickness, trauma, financial hardship, breakups, and unemployment, it can make it difficult to find a reason to be thankful or to have gratitude. There is always something to be grateful for because God is always there for us and working on our behalf.

As we pray with a heart of gratitude, we can see the light in the darkness and recognize God's fingerprints on all His great gifts to us. Praying with a heart of gratitude makes God's works more visible. Gratitude shrinks our entitlement, selfishness, pride, and despair. God is so good that He designed gratitude to bring us closer to Him, improve our relationships with others, grow us as a people, and increase the quality of our lives.

Seeds to Plant, Water, and Ruminate:
Whether we are on a mountain top or a valley, God is deserving of our gratitude.

Prayer for Growth

Dear Gracious God,

You are wonderful in all of Your ways. You are worthy of all the glory, honor, and praise. God You are holy, perfect, and full of light. Your power and love are unmatched and uncontested. There is no one greater than You. I cannot comprehend the magnitude of Your domination, nor the loveliness and complexity of Your being.

You are the Author of Truth and the Arbiter of Justice. I'm undeserving of Your forgiveness and blessings, yet You give them to me freely. Thank You for Your mercy, kindness, and salvation.

In Jesus' name, amen.

Day 7: What Do I Pray About?

Part 7: Health and Safety

Growth Scriptures:

"The angel of the Lord encamps around those who fear him, and delivers them."
-Psalm 34: 7 RSV

"He went around all of Galilee, teaching in their synagogues, proclaiming the gospel of the kingdom, and curing every disease and illness among the people."
- Matthew 4:23 NAB

Growth Insight: God is a healer and protector. The Bible tells us that God even keeps us from dangers that are unknown to us. He protected Daniel in the lions' den and prevented the furnace flames from engulfing Shadrach, Meshach, and Abed-nego. God saved Paul from his three shipwrecks and used a large sea creature to rescue Jonah when he was thrown overboard. Jesus calmed the storm and the waters while He and the disciples were on the ship. God is able to protect us and our loved ones in the middle of war zones, natural disasters, vehicles accidents, high crime areas, and so on. Jesus healed people with all types of mental health and physical health conditions.

The Holy Spirit empowered the apostles to heal in the New Testament and our Heavenly Father enabled the prophets to heal in the Old Testament. Paul instructed the early church Christians to go to the church elders for healing. God can use doctors and other healthcare professionals to heal us as well. God still does miracles, and we are safe in His arms. Even when we do leave this earth, we transition securely into His heavenly kingdom.

When negative things do happen, God has allowed it for purposes that are not always known to us, but He is still in control. God listens to our petitions and our prayers do make a difference. God intervenes on our behalf within the confines of His divine plan, love, and wisdom.

Seeds to Plant, Water, and Ruminate:
God is my place of refuge and recuperation.

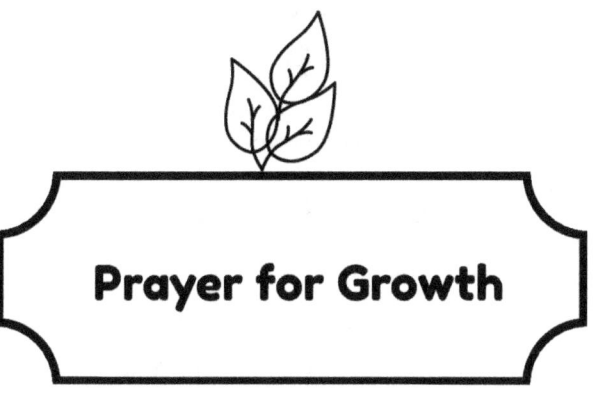

Prayer for Growth

Dear Lord,

You are Yahweh Rapha and Elohim Shomri, my healer and protector. I entrust my life and wellbeing to You. You alone can save and shield me. I lift my loved ones up to You and ask that You guard their minds, strengthen their faith, heal their bodies, and keep them safe from danger. Guide my feet on the path I should take. Thank You for Your strength, power, and love.

In Jesus' name, I pray. Amen.

Prayer Challenge: Week 13

Pray About Your Mental Health

The rationale behind the challenge:

Mental health is a critical component of our spiritual growth. When our mental health conditions go untreated, our spiritual health declines. Depression makes it difficult for us to comprehend and believe God's promises and truth about Him, ourselves, and our situations. Anxiety and trauma rob us of peace and joy. These conditions constrict our vision and trust in God. Hallucinations distort our reality and the ability to discern God's voice. ADHD and bipolar disorders affect our ability to control our impulses and focus on God's Word.

The intention of this challenge is to bring awareness to the necessity of requesting God to intervene when we are struggling with poor mental health and how it can negatively impact our spiritual growth. Any of these issues can prevent us from feeling close to God, receiving His truth, learning more about Him, obeying His Word, loving Him and others, worshiping Him, using our gifts, and understanding our worth and purpose. However, when we lean on God for strength, hope, truth, and healing, we will experience a sense of gratitude, love, intimacy, empowerment, compassion, forgiveness, and grace that we never thought was possible.

Growth Scripture:

"For God has not given us a spirit of fear, but of power and of love and of a sound mind."
-2 Timothy 1:7 NKJV

Day 1: Anxiety, Worry, and Fear

Growth Scriptures:

"Casting all your cares [all your anxieties, all your worries, and all your concerns, once and for all] on Him, for He cares about you [with deepest affection, and watches over you very carefully]."
-1 Peter 5:7 AMP

"And which of you by worrying can add even one hour to his life?"
-Matthew 6:27 NET

"When I worried about many things, your assuring words soothed my soul."
-Psalm 94:19 GW

Growth Insight: The world around us may seem dangerous at times and the issues of life tend to pile up. Sometimes we become concerned about the wellbeing of those we love or regarding situations we do not want to confront. Other times, there are jobs we don't want to lose, interactions we don't want to mess up, people we don't want to disappoint, health reports we are too anxious to read, places we're too afraid to go, and opportunities we're scared to pursue. We also fear that our needs and wants won't be met in our relationships, friendships, careers, and finances. All these fears and worries are common. That's why God the Father, Jesus, and angels tell believers numerous times in the Scriptures to not worry or be afraid. Things that happen to us may be out of our control, but worry and fear are optional.

Worry can be crippling and prevent us from enjoying life, experiencing emotional peace and freedom, sleeping, taking advantage of opportunities, building relationships, going on adventures, socializing, and leaving the house. Worrying is unproductive and will not change anything. Give all your anxiety, worry, and fear over to God because He cares about You. He has the power to change the situation and your perspective of it. Have faith that God is in control and that the Holy Spirit will help you.

Seeds to Plant, Water, and Ruminate:
If Christ can raise the dead, walk on water, calm the stormy sea, and heal the inflicted, then He can alleviate my fear, worry, and anxiety.

Prayer for Growth

Dear God,

Thank You for easing my burdens and relieving my anxieties. When life seems frightening and my life is in disarray, remind me that You are a God of order and omnipotence. When I'm filled with doubts and fears, reassure me of Your promises and truth. When worry stifles me, free me with Your peace. Grant me the wisdom and courage to be proactive and manage the things within my control. Allow me to let go of the things outside of my control and trustingly place them into Your hands.

In Jesus' mighty name, amen.

Day 2: Depression

Growth Scriptures:

"Come to me, all you that are weary and are carrying heavy burdens, and I will give you rest."
-Matthew 11:28 NRSV

"And the peace of God, which surpasses all understanding, will guard your hearts and your minds in Christ Jesus. Finally, brothers, whatever is true, whatever is honorable, whatever is right, whatever is pure, whatever is lovely, whatever is admirable—if anything is excellent or praiseworthy—think on these things."
-Philippians 4:7-8 MSB

Growth Insight: Depression is a heavy burden to bear, and you're not meant to carry it alone. Despite that fact, many of us try to hide depression due to shame or hopelessness. God is our ever-present helper, but He also provides practical resources to support us through difficult times. Therapy, support groups, family, friends, prescribed medications, self-help books, and mental health tools can all be part of His provision. It may be difficult for others to comprehend depression unless they've experienced it themselves, so don't be discouraged when some people are not supportive in the way you need. Many of us have been taught that it is a sin to be depressed, that we lack the faith to be healed, or we're a bad Christian if we experience depression. None of these misguided notions are true. Using these resources is not a sign of weak faith or that we are failing as a Christian; it is often one of the many ways God extends His grace, comfort, and healing to us.

Sometimes we falsely believe that we have to be flawless super-Christians in order for God to love us, please Him, or be used by Him. Contrarily, Jesus is empathetic towards us, and the Holy Spirit is close to us and there to comfort those in despair. In the Bible, Job, David, Jeremiah, Hannah, Naomi, Elijah, and Solomon all struggled with depression, yet they are regarded as great people of faith. God used them when they were broken, and He can do the same for you. Depression manifests itself in many ways, and it infects our mind, body, and soul. We must surrender every aspect of ourselves and our lives to God and to the truth presented in His Word.

Seeds to Plant, Water, and Ruminate:

God can pour into the empty, heal the afflicted, mold the broken into something new, find the lost, strengthen the weak, and comfort the brokenhearted.

Prayer for Growth

Dear God of Peace and Mercy,

All praise and glory to Your name. Thank You for being there during my mental anguish, dark days, and sleepless nights. Use Your Word to lead me to the truth about my identity, worth, and life circumstances. Remind me to be patient as I wait to be healed. Shine the light of truth on the lies society, friends, family, social media, novels, songs, movies, videos, and television have told me over the years. It took time to develop these beliefs and negative thoughts, and it will take time to replace them with truth. Help me to realize that You can heal me from depression no matter how long I have suffered from it or how many times I have regressed. Give me courage to hope in You and seek the resources that I need.

I ask these things in Jesus' powerful name, amen.

Day 3: Trauma

Growth Scriptures:

"'No weapon formed against you shall prosper, and you will refute every tongue that accuses you. This is the heritage of the servants of the LORD, and their vindication is from Me,' declares the LORD."
-Isaiah 54:17 BSB

"You plotted evil against me, but God turned it into good, in order to preserve the lives of many people who are alive today because of what happened."
-Genesis 50:20 GNT

Growth Insight: Since the downfall of Adam and Eve in the garden of Eden, there has been a downward spiral of calamity, sin, pain, and confusion. Horrible things happen that were not in God's original intent and will for mankind. At some point in your life, it is likely that you will experience at least one traumatic event. Whether you are an adult or a child, there are situations that can be so disturbing that they have a long-lasting, negative emotional impact. Being a witness to or a victim of a robbery, murder, vehicle accident, natural disaster, war, physical attack, abuse (sexual, physical, emotional, verbal), kidnapping, or physical injury are all too common examples of potentially traumatizing occurrences. Just because things of a traumatic nature take place does not mean that you will be automatically traumatized from them. Trauma occurs when life-threatening or emotionally disturbing events take place that exceed our tools and capabilities to process the event in a healthy manner and successfully self-soothe. Situations like these make prayer even more essential. We have to pray for God to send comfort, support from others, emotional wellbeing, and a healthy perspective regarding what transpired. God is able and willing to heal and bring us out of the worst suffering and circumstances.

Seeds to Plant, Water, and Ruminate:
There are things the Enemy hoped would completely break and devastate me. Then God used the situations to strengthen me, help me grow, bring me closer to Him, help others, and to see blessings come from it that couldn't be fathomed or predicted.

Day 4: Grief

Growth Scriptures:

"The Lord is near to the brokenhearted, and saves the crushed in spirit."
-Psalm 34:18 RSV

"And he said, 'Where have you laid him?' They said to him, 'Lord, come and see.' Jesus wept."
-John 11:34-35 RSV

Growth Insight: There is no one-size-fits-all approach to grieving. It looks different for everyone, and there is no magical cutoff point. Grief can initially feel as though your breath has been taken away and your world has stopped. You may feel angry that life appears to continue as normal for the rest of the world. Some people blame themselves, others, God, or the one who died for the death. Shock and disbelief of what has occurred is also common. Others may attempt to make bargains with God or others that they'll do life differently if their loved one could be brought back. Sorrow, emptiness, regret, despair, numbness, loss of identity, and wondering if you could have prevented the death somehow can also be a part of grief. Don't judge yourself for having these thoughts and emotions or try to push them away. Acknowledge your feelings, but don't try to hold on to them. Let the waves of emotion come and go.

No one is immune to grief. Even Jesus wept when his friend Lazarus died. Accepting the death of a loved one is a painful process. Remember, Jesus sent the Holy Spirit to comfort us, and He deeply empathizes with our pain. Engaging in activities our loved ones enjoyed, such as eating their favorite foods, traveling to meaningful places, listening to their favorite music, watching their favorite shows, or continuing their hobbies, can help us feel connected to them. We can also honor their memory by reminiscing with others, looking through photos, writing, creating art, keeping sentimental items, organizing a dedication ceremony, praying, practicing self-care, doing mindfulness activities, joining a support group, or seeking therapy. Each of these can help us process our grief and begin to create a new sense of normalcy.

Prayer for Growth

Dear Loving and Merciful God,

I come to You with a contrite heart. I know that You help those who are hurting and heavy burdened. You feel anger towards injustice and empathize with those who are distressed and frightened. Lord, I ask that you alleviate my fears, guard my dreams, resolve my guilt, and heal my emotional anguish. Take my turmoil and turn it into hope, peace, and joy. Shine Your light of truth on any unhealthy thoughts that arise. Although I have struggled to see the good and to understand Your plan, I trust You. Help me to feel Your presence and see Your glory through the darkness.

I pray these in Jesus' name, amen.

Seeds to Plant, Water, and Ruminate:
The Lord is there beside me as I grieve.

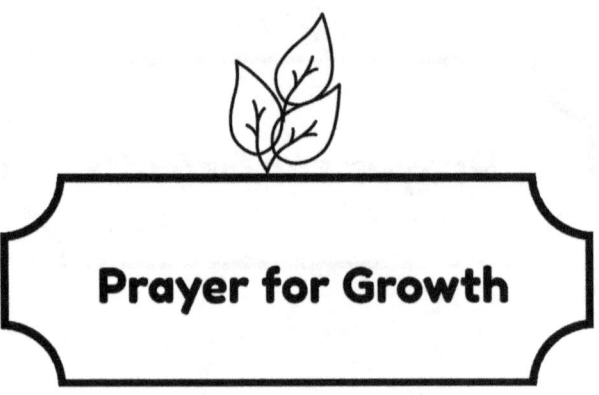

Prayer for Growth

Dear Triune God,

You are El Roi, the God who sees me. You are Elohim Imi, the God who is with me. You empathize with my pain and tears. Please wrap Your compassionate arms around me as You strengthen and console me. Let Your Spirit that dwells within me fill me will joy and hope. Provide me with the peace that only You can supply. I need You on the mountain top and in the valley. I praise You in the sun and in the storm. Thank You for Your mercy and kindness.

In Jesus' name, I pray. Amen.

Day 5: Life Transitions

Growth Scriptures:

"For everything there is a season, and a time for every purpose under heaven: a time to be born, and a time to die; a time to plant, and a time to pluck up that which is planted; a time to kill, and a time to heal; a time to break down, and a time to build up; a time to weep, and a time to laugh; a time to mourn, and a time to dance."
-Ecclesiastes 3:1-4 ASV

"Behold, I will do a new thing. It springs out now. Don't you know it? I will even make a way in the wilderness, and rivers in the desert."
-Isaiah 43:19 WEB

Growth Insight: Whether or not we are excited, dreading it, or ready, change happens. It doesn't matter if the circumstances are good or bad, nothing stays the same forever. As people, we age and mature. Time is fleeting and emotions fluctuate. People and possessions come and go. We relocate, pursue dreams and adventure, settle down, lose jobs, get promotions, improve health, decline in heath, expand our families, experience empty nest, lose loved ones, deal with mental and physical limitations, retire, start our careers, end relationships, and begin new relationships. We succeed and fail. Trouble and conflicts rise up and resolve.

We must embrace that everything is temporary. Find ways to manage the unpleasant times and fully enjoy the good times. Don't take people, opportunities, advantages, luxuries, or God's grace for granted. Rely on God and trust Him to get you through difficult life transitions. Thank Him for the positive changes. When you pray, ask God what He wants you to take away from each experience. Through prayer, God can change our attitudes, hearts, and perspectives regarding any given situation.

Seeds to Plant, Water, and Ruminate:
It's okay to reminisce about the past, look forward to the future, and to grieve or celebrate the moment. However, don't get stuck in any moment; life moves on.

Prayer for Growth

Dear Lord,

Even when my life seems out of control, I know You are in control. Hold me under your umbrella of protection when life's chaotic storms rage. Thank You for new beginnings and for the chapters that come to an end. Help me to live in the moment instead of the past and the future. Because of the hope I have in You, I can face any challenge or change that comes my way. I know You are with me through the highs and the lows. Help me to see how You have used my circumstances for good.

In Jesus' name, amen.

Day 6: Coping Skills and Self-care

Growth Scriptures:

"There were so many people coming and going that Jesus and his disciples didn't even have time to eat. So he said to them, 'Let us go off by ourselves to some place where we will be alone and you can rest a while.'"
-Mark 6:31 GNT

"But Jesus Himself would often slip away to the wilderness and pray."
-Luke 5:16 NASB

Growth Insight: Developing and applying coping skills and self-care routines into our daily lives is essential to our spiritual growth and overall wellbeing. Self-care means doing things that help to improve or sustain our spiritual, mental, and physical health. Coping skills are actions we take to manage stressful situations and difficult feelings in a healthy manner. Self-care is more connected to the prevention and management of mental disorders and health conditions. Coping skills are more commonly associated with reacting to emotionally triggering circumstances.

Activities such as reading the Bible, praying, taking a nature walk, exercising, eating healthily, journaling, listening to music, engaging in mindfulness activities, starting a new hobby, sightseeing, taking time off, volunteering, creating art, listening to Christian podcasts and sermons, confiding in someone, taking a bubble bath, or gardening can help to nourish our mind, body, and spirit. In order to be the best we can be, we cannot neglect to take care of ourselves. Regularly practicing self-care and coping skills enable us to effectively carry out our duties, help others, and serve God. Others around us can also learn how to cope and manage their wellbeing by observing us. Let's set a good example and assist one another through life.

Seeds to Plant, Water, and Ruminate:
If I don't take care of myself, then I eventually won't be of much good to myself or others. Jesus modeled self-care and taught it to His disciples.

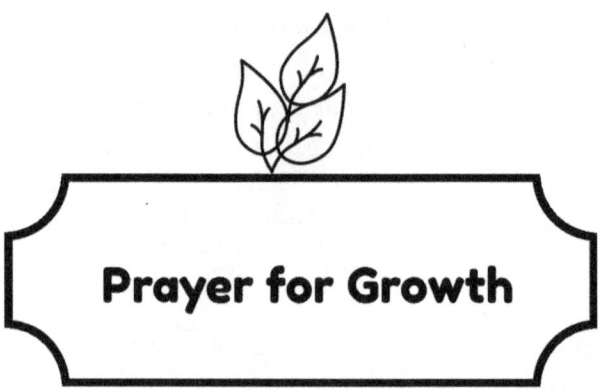

Prayer for Growth

Dear Lord,

You are my lighthouse and lightening rod. Thank You for being the Good Shepherd and caring for me. Teach me how to navigate through the storms of life and manage the strikes and waves. Direct me to tools that effectively help me to cope with my emotions, triggers, and undesirable circumstances. Instruct me so that I learn to discern how and when to be proactive with self-care.

I pray these things in Jesus' name, amen.

Day 7: Anger, Resentment, and Unforgiveness

Growth Scriptures:

"Let all bitterness, anger and wrath, shouting and slander be removed from you, along with all malice. And be kind and compassionate to one another, forgiving one another, just as God also forgave you in Christ."
-Ephesians 4:31-32 CSB

"Be angry but do not sin; do not let the sun set on your anger, and do not leave room for the devil."
-Ephesians 4:26-27 NAB

"Understand this, my dear brothers and sisters! Let every person be quick to listen, slow to speak, slow to anger. For human anger does not accomplish God's righteousness."
-James 1:19-20 NET

Growth Insight: Being quick to anger, holding onto resentment, and refusing to forgive is exhausting, painful, and self-destructive. It's like willfully choosing to pick up a load of heavy bricks each day and carry it with you throughout every circumstance. Although our reasons for experiencing these feelings may be understandable or justifiable, we have to learn to let them go so that they don't consume us. Sometimes we harbor anger towards others who may be completely unaware or unconcerned about the negative impact it has on us. Unbeknownst to them, we are trapped in time and misery while they continue on with their lives.

Forgiveness does not mean that you minimize the impact and severity of what people did or that you approve of what they did. Forgiving someone does not make you weak or a doormat. We can forgive and still set healthy boundaries. Forgiveness means that you will not continually attempt to hold their transgression over their head, repeatedly punish them for the same offense, treat them poorly, have bitterness towards them, or wish them ill-will. Forgiveness is not for them; it is to free you. It may initially seem unjust or despicable, but in the end, it feels so good and liberating to release the heavy load. If nothing else convicts your heart to forgive, remember that we are commanded to forgive because God has forgiven us.

Seeds to Plant, Water, and Ruminate:
I'll forgive because God says so. I'll forgive whether or not I deem the other person worthy or not. I'll forgive because I'm worthy to be free from the chains of unforgiveness, anger, bitterness, and resentment.

Prayer for Growth

Dear Savior and Redeemer,

I owe my life to You. Thank You for forgiving me of all my sins and gifting me with salvation. Help me to forgive others and to display empathy and compassion. Lord, holding onto anger and unforgiveness is detrimental to my soul, spirit, and wellbeing. I fear that I will be perceived as weak, send out an open invitation to be hurt again, or be taken advantage of if I forgive. Forgiveness feels as though my suffering is being minimized and the other person faces no consequences for his or her actions. Grant me with emotional healing and strengthen me to be obedient to Your command to forgive. Help me to not be easily angered.

In Jesus' name, amen.

Prayer Challenge: Week 14

Discover Your Answered Prayers

The rationale behind the challenge:

The purpose of this challenge is for you to re-examine prayers that you perceived to have possibly gone unanswered. God might answer our prayers in a way that seems unconventional, unexpected, or unfavorable, but that doesn't mean that He doesn't answer our prayer requests. Unfortunately, some people believe that just because God did not answer their prayers in a seemingly more desirable manner, or in the way they expected, that He did not answer their prayer at all. Prayer requires a measure of faith that God is in control and that his plan is for our benefit, benefit of others, and for His glory. During this week's challenge, we will study the different methods God utilized to respond to the prayers of biblical figures. As we gain a better understanding of prayer, our confusion, doubt, fear, anger, disappointment, and resentment dissipates. Those feelings will gradually be replaced with increased trust, faith, wellbeing, and thankfulness. A change in your perspective regarding prayer signifies growth.

Growth Scripture and Grow Quote:

"'For my thoughts are not your thoughts, neither are your ways my ways,' declares the LORD. 'As the heavens are higher than the earth, so are my ways higher than your ways and my thoughts than your thoughts.'"
-Isaiah 55:8-9 NIV

"If God seems slow in responding, it is because He is preparing a better gift. He will not deny us. God withholds what you are not yet ready for. He wants you to have a lively desire for His greatest gifts. All of which is to say, pray always and do not lose heart. "
-St. Augustine

Day 1: How Does God Answer Prayers?

Part 1: Messengers

Growth Scriptures:

"And afterward, I will pour out My Spirit on all people. Your sons and daughters will prophesy, your old men will dream dreams, your young men will see visions."
-Joel 2:28 MSB

"In times past, God spoke in partial and various ways to our ancestors through the prophets."
-Hebrews 1:1 NAB

Growth Insight 1: God may communicate with you by sending a messenger or leading you towards wise counsel. There are examples in Scripture that detail events of God sending angels and prophets to give messages to His people. For instance, God sent Gabriel to inform Mary that she would give birth to Jesus and to Zachariah to notify him of Elizabeth's pregnancy. Jonah was sent to warn the people of Nineveh to repent. Isaiah was sent to proclaim to Hezekiah that God would save the city from the Assyrians, and that instead of Hezekiah dying of his illness, fifteen years would be added to his life.

Even today, there are many reports of individuals being approached by strangers to reveal a message from God to a specific person. These individuals may confirm what you have been perceiving to be God's will or disclose a vision of something yet to come into fruition in your life. Also, you may turn on the television or attend a worship service, and the minister may preach a sermon that speaks directly to your situation. Additionally, wise counsel may present itself to you in the form of medical personnel, mental health professionals, advisors, consultants, mentors, close friends, support group members, colleagues, clergy, or instructors. For this reason, we should surround ourselves with godly individuals who have proven themselves trustworthy with God's Word.

Seeds to Plant, Water, and Ruminate:
To give us a revelation, God may send someone to us seemingly out of the blue or a person that we least expect to hear from.

Prayer for Growth

Dear Lord,

You are not a God of confusion. You are truth and light. Lord, we thank You for sending people to us that help bring us clarity on what You require of us, how You are going to bless us, or how You are going to use us. Grant me wisdom to discern Your true messengers from those who intend to be deceptive. I open my heart to You and Your Word. Let Your will be done.

In Jesus' name, amen.

Day 2: How Does God Answer Prayers?

Part 2: Dreams

Growth Scriptures:

"He said, 'Now hear my words. If there is a prophet among you, I, Yahweh, will make myself known to him in a vision. I will speak with him in a dream.'"
-Numbers 12:6 WEB

"Then, being divinely warned in a dream that they should not return to Herod, they departed for their own country another way. Now when they had departed, behold, an angel of the Lord appeared to Joseph in a dream, saying, 'Arise, take the young Child and His mother, flee to Egypt, and stay there until I bring you word; for Herod will seek the young Child to destroy Him.'"
-Matthew 2:13 NKJV

Growth Insight 2: God may reply to you or reveal His will for you in a dream. Dreams are often complex and can be difficult to interpret. Some dreams expose our worries, fears, and desires. Other dreams are attempts to process negative and positive events that have occurred in our lives. Nonetheless, God will occasionally, show you a glimpse of something you or your children may achieve, warn you to stay away from something nefarious, give you peace about an unresolved issue, give you direction on what path to take, and more.

The Bible records God speaking to various individuals through dreams. God revealed to Joseph (son of Jacob) that he would hold a high position of authority over others. He disclosed to Nebuchadnezzar that his kingdom was coming to an end, and to Jacob that he and his descendants would possess the land of Israel. In the New Testament, God conveyed to Joseph that he was to flee to Egypt with Jesus and Mary. Solomon asked God to provide him with wisdom to preside judgment over the kingdom and to teach him right from wrong. God was pleased with his request and responded to Solomon in a dream. In addition to wisdom, God blessed Solomon with things not requested, such as wealth and honor. Dreams are one of many pathways God uses to communicate with His creation.

Seeds to Plant, Water, and Ruminate:
God can speak to me in my dreams.

Prayer for Growth

Dear God,

Thank You for keeping watch over me while I sleep. I pray that You infiltrate my dreams with good things. Guard my mind and spirit as I rest. If You wish to communicate with me while I sleep, please make it plain or send an interpreter to me who is empowered by the Holy Spirit.

In Jesus' name, amen.

Day 3: How Does God Answer Prayers?

Part 3: Scripture

Growth Scriptures:

"The LORD's precepts are fair and make one joyful. The LORD's commands are pure and give insight for life."
-Psalm 19:8 NET

"Call to me, and I will answer you; I will tell you great things beyond the reach of your knowledge."
-Jeremiah 33:3 NAB

Growth Insight 3: After praying, you may be led to a certain biblical passage that provides insight into your particular situation. The Scriptures are filled with wisdom, commands, moral lessons, and practical takeaways. No matter how many times you read a particular verse, the Holy Spirit can lead you to a fresh realization in the moment. During different seasons in our lives, some verses have greater impact on us than others. Sometimes we brush over Scriptures and do not fully grasp the power or significance of them at the time. As we grow in our spiritual journey, we may come to understand things we were not able to comprehend when we were younger or new in our faith. Ask God to lead you to the right verse that directs you to the answer or encouragement that you need.

Seeds to Plant, Water, and Ruminate:
Prayer and Scripture nourish my mind, soul and spirit. They change my heart, stimulate my growth, and dictate my course of action.

Prayer for Growth

Dear Lord,

I am grateful for Your holy Scripture and pray that I will always find delight in Your Word. You have provided me with the gift of prayer and a Bible that provides insight into Your will for my life. Thank You for providing a glimpse into who You are through Your Word. I desire to look to Your Word for answers instead of being influenced by ungodly sources or misguided individuals. When I am experiencing difficulty understanding what to do, lead me to Your Word for clarification. Instead of consulting You last, incline my heart to seek You first for help, hope, guidance, and clarity. Enable me to abide, recall, cherish, and respect Your authoritative Word.

In Jesus' name, amen.

Day 4: How Does God Answer Prayers?

Part 4: Closed Doors

Growth Scripture:

"To the angel of the church in Philadelphia write: These are the words of the One who is holy and true, who holds the key of David. What He opens no one can shut (except Him who opens) and no one can open."
-Revelation 3:7 MSB

Growth Insight 4: God tries to communicate to us through various means, but sometimes we just don't get it. If there were flashing lights, arrows, and whistles, we would still miss it. It's occurrences like these when adopting what I call a "closed-door policy" may be helpful. That is, asking God to close the doors that we were not meant to go through or bring ill-advised opportunities to an end. If it's a temptation that we're struggling with, then we may beseech God to take away our access to it or desire for it. When you can't hear His whisper, the dreams have ceased, the Scripture seems ambiguous on the topic, and friends have no revelation, then we can petition that God take away all the paths and choices that are not meant for us. We can pray that God leaves open the doors that lead to growth and blessings, and that He closes the doors that lead to death, confusion, disobedience, and sin.

Seeds to Plant, Water, and Ruminate:
When I can't discern God's will, I can ask Him to close the door if it's not meant for me.

Prayer for Growth

Dear Lord,

Thank You for making a way for me when I see no way. Thank You for closing the doors that are not to my benefit and opening doors to spiritual maturation, purpose, blessings, and service to You. Provide me with the courage and wisdom to seize the opportunities that will prosper me and to turn away from the options that lead to sin, harm, and regression. Reinforce my trust in You and increase my dependence on You. Let me look to Your truth and Your strength as I face temptation.

I pray these things in Jesus' name, amen.

Day 5: How Does God Answer Prayers?

Part 5: Materialization

Growth Scriptures:

"Ask and it will be given to you; seek and you will find; knock and the door will be opened for you."
-Matthew 7:7 NET

"Before they call, I will answer; while they are yet speaking, I will hear."
-Isaiah 65:24 NAB

Growth Insight 5: God may choose to answer your prayer by actually materializing what you prayed for. That is, we may experience the emotional or physical healing that we asked for. We may witness God soften the hearts of our spouse or children after we petitioned for conflict resolution or for them to accept the Lord as Savior. When we are down to our last dime, we may receive the job we requested or an unexpected check in the mail. In Scripture, we see battles won, demons expelled, women conceive, provisions made, guidance provided, hearts comforted, hope restored, and forgiveness granted after believers prayed. Through prayer, we are able to witness the growth in ourselves and others. When God answers our prayers, we should look for the lesson, express gratitude, and acknowledge God's glory that shines through the situation.

Seeds to Plant, Water, and Ruminate:
God answers my prayers with things that are for my good.

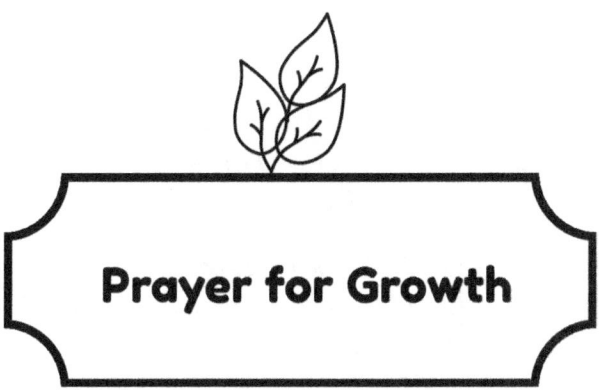

Prayer for Growth

Dear Lord,

You are the ultimate provider and my shepherd. You meet all of my needs. Thank You for blessing me with great gifts. Help me to not take these things for granted or to value them more than You. Thank You for allowing me to recognize my answered prayers. Open my eyes to the prayers You have answered that I have yet to comprehend.

In Jesus' name, amen.

Day 6: What If I Don't Get the Answer I Want?

Growth Scriptures and Growth Quote:

"Trust in the Lord with all of your heart; do not depend on your own understanding."
- Proverbs 3:5 NLT

"For the LORD God is a sun and shield: the LORD will give grace and glory: no good thing will he withhold from them that walk uprightly."
-Psalm 84:11 KJV

"We must not think that God takes no notice of us, when He does not answer our wishes: for He has a right to distinguish what we actually need."
-John Calvin

Growth Insight: God is not a genie in the bottle or a wishing well. We are not entitled to get everything we want nor is God obligated to do so. Our sovereign Lord has the right to tell us "no" or to "wait." Remember that we do serve a loving, compassionate, just, gracious, wise, and omniscient God. When we do not get the answer we want, we must learn to trust Him. Resist the urge to become angry, resentful, fearful, dejected, or hopeless. God is in control and has a plan for you to succeed and grow—not to be irreparably harmed and fail. Scripture says that He will not withhold any good thing from those who do what is right. If He says "no," then it's not what's best for you or in His will for you.

It can be painful to accept God's answer in the moment, but God will eventually reveal the light at the end of the tunnel. We cannot see the full picture like God can. There may be a time when you look back and thank God that He did not give you what you asked for because it would have led to a disastrous end. When God says "no," He either has something better in store for you or has to take you a different route to ensure that you are strengthened and grow. Sometimes God will do more for us than we even thought to ask for or could imagine, but we must wait. God has perfect timing. Thus, when He tells us to wait, it is for our good and/or the good of the others around us.

Seeds to Plant, Water, and Ruminate:
Like a good parent, God does not give us everything we want but provides all that we need. We are not entitled to anything, but out of His love and compassion, God blesses us with great things.

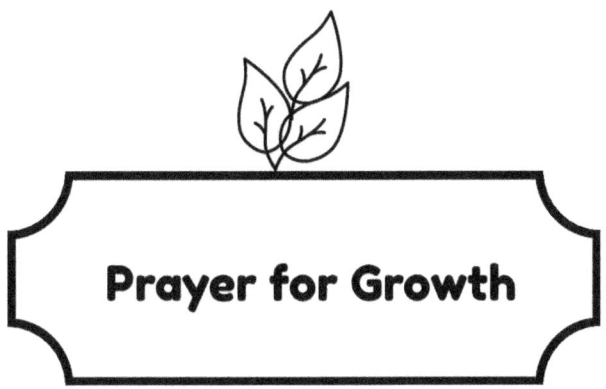

Prayer for Growth

Dear Heavenly Father,

Thank You for Your great gifts and Your compassion. You are a good Father who provides, protects, and instructs. Help me to see the mercy, grace, and blessings that are in progress when You do not answer my requests in the way that I was anticipating. Comfort me while I await Your revelation and aid. Remind me of the vastness of Your good judgement and wisdom. Help me to trust You and to feel Your love for me.

In Jesus' name, amen.

Day 7: Does God Ignore Prayers?

Growth Scriptures:

"If I cherished sin in my heart, the Lord wouldn't have listened."
-Psalm 66:18 WEB

"We know that God does not listen to sinners, but he does listen to one who worships him and obeys his will."
-John 9:31 NRSV

"For the eyes of the Lord are on the righteous, and his ears are open to their prayer. But the face of the Lord is against those who do evil."
-1 Peter 3:12 ESV

Growth Insight: As believers, God may not grant all our requests, but He always responds to our prayers. He may not answer our prayers at the time we want Him to, or in the manner we are expecting, but God answers us. God knows the things that we cannot foresee or comprehend. Thus, we must trust that when our petitions are denied that it is for our good and His glory. He knows what's best for us and has a plan for our lives.

However, God is listening; but this means that He will not give consideration to their requests if their hearts are not humbled and their motives are impure. We must be in submission to God and in line with His will in order to receive what we are asking for. Requests from a heart filled with resentment, contempt, cynicism, disrespect, and disobedience towards God will not be honored. Prayers submitted to God with a humble and sincere heart are not in vain; He will hear and answer you.

Seeds to Plant, Water, and Ruminate:
God may answer with a *yes*, *no*, or *wait*, but He always answers me.

Prayer for Growth

Dear Triune God,

You are the Ruler of Heaven and Earth, yet I am in Your thoughts. You assign me worth. You are attentive to the most minute detail of my life and the most subatomic aspect of the universe. Although I am undeserving, You entertain my prayers and grace me with Your response. Thank You for not being a God who is unconcerned with His creation. Thank You for every blessing and every prayer that You answered regardless of whether You answered it with a *no, yes,* or *not yet.* Remind me that all things work together for the good of those who love You. Thank You for Your mercy, grace, and forgiveness.

In Jesus' mighty name, I pray. Amen.

Prayer for Continual Spiritual Growth

Dear God of Heaven and Earth,

Thank You for allowing me to take part in this incredible spiritual growth journey. I pray that I continue to seek You with my whole heart and worship You in Your rightful position. Let me not place any sin, desire, person, profession, ambition, societal influence, or possession above You. Give me courage to serve You boldly and to utilize the spiritual gifts, talents, strengths, and skills You have bestowed upon me. Make Your vision plain to me and grant me an obedience heart. Protect my mind against the lies of the Enemy. Lord, forgive all of my trespasses against You and turn my heart away from sin. Empower me to resist temptation and break every stronghold that plagues me. When I disobey the commands that You have given, remind me of Your love and grace so that I am equipped and encouraged to return to the right path immediately. I long for You and need You every moment of the day. Let me not seek You in prayer only when I'm in need, rather enable me to communicate with You throughout the day. Help me to crave You and Your Word and to delight in reading Your holy Scripture.

In Jesus' magnificent and holy name, amen.

www.ingramcontent.com/pod-product-compliance
Lightning Source LLC
Chambersburg PA
CBHW021147160426
43194CB00007B/726